HEAR THEIR VOICES

A Portrait of An American Foster Family

HARMONY KLINGENMEYER

Trilogy Christian Publishers
A Wholly Owned Subsidiary of Trinity Broadcasting Network
2442 Michelle Drive
Tustin, CA 92780

For information, address Trilogy Christian Publishing
Rights Department, 2442 Michelle Drive, Tustin, Ca 92780.

Trilogy Christian Publishing/ TBN and colophon are trademarks of
Trinity Broadcasting Network.

For information about special discounts for bulk purchases, please
contact Trilogy Christian Publishing.

Manufactured in the United States of America

10 9 8 7 6 5 4 3 2 1

Library of Congress Cataloging-in-Publication Data is available.
ISBN 978-1-64088-413-7
ISBN 978-1-64088-414-4

Dedication

My Father, Dan Ramsey:

He has shown you, O man, what is good;
And what does the Lord require of you
But to do justly, To love mercy, And to walk
humbly with your God?

Micah 6:8

You have shown me, Dad.

Table of Contents

I Dare You

A day came, a day when Brenden no longer screamed out in terror in the middle of the night. A day came when he no longer used obscenities to get his way or beat his head against the wall. He no longer bit and scratched himself or others. A day came on which my son experienced peace. And on that day he said to me:

"Mom, I think I'm full of God."

"Yes, Son, you are," I replied. After a moment, I turned to him and asked, "Why did you tell me that?"

"Because," he said, "When I worship Jesus, I hear God's voice. He reminds me of all the times He protected me. I tell people how I could have died, how I was homeless, and God rescued me. I know I am full of God because I hear Him speak."

I could barely converse through the tears, but I managed to say, "You are so right, Son. You *are* full of God."

When people ask me why we chose this life, my story begins, not with infertility, not with a desire to be a mother, not with Scott's Klinefelter Syndrome. Those things fade in comparison to the grand reason. The reason we chose this life is because our hearts burned for a generation of fatherless sons.

OUR PROPHETIC LOVE STORY

Scott and I met online and were nearly inseparable from our

first date. Three days after meeting him, I was sitting in my cousin's living room, describing the man of my dreams to some of my family. Out of my mouth I spoke the words that would become the banner of our marriage:

"Scott is called to be a father to a generation of fatherless sons."

At that moment, I recognized that my words were prophetic, that God had used my mouth to release destiny, and in that moment I knew that Scott and I would be married and spend our lives together. What I had no idea of at the time was that Scott was not able to father children naturally. Klinefelter Syndrome had stolen that possibility and left Scott feeling worthless and listless. Because of the shortness of our courtship, he had not shared that very private bit of information with me. God's intention for Scott, however, was far greater than he or I could have imagined in that moment. And Klinefelter Syndrome could not stop what God had purposed.

About a month into our relationship, Scott and I were out for dinner. I felt the Holy Spirit nudge me to share the prophetic word that I had released at my cousin's home. I took his hand and said, "I'm going to tell you something that might sound weird, but I need to say it anyway. God sometimes tells me amazing things about people. I feel so blessed that I get to share His heart with others, and, well, He told me something about you."

"What is it?" Scott asked.

"He told me you are called to be a father to a generation of fatherless sons."

Scott looked down at his plate. I could tell he was feeling some strong emotions. My husband does not enjoy being emotional, but he looked up at me with red eyes and said, "I have to tell you something, too. I am not physically able to father children."

"Well, that doesn't matter," I said, almost laughing. Was that all he was worried about? "God didn't say you would SIRE

2

a generation of fatherless sons. He said you would FATHER a generation of fatherless sons. Look around. This world is full of children with missing dads. You are called to step into the void left by absentee fathers and release identity over young men in a way that only a father can."

Scott looked at me as if he wished what I said was true, but he did not truly believe it. I just smiled and nodded. "Don't worry," I said. "It's God's job to perform His Word and it's our job to believe it. Just believe with me and God will do the rest."

Fast forward with me a year and a half later. It was November 2011, and Scott and I had been married about a month. I was working for a timeshare company at the time, booking tours of their property. I was good at it, and had been awarded Marketer of the Year for two years in a row. A woman walked up to me with a baby in her arms and a girl who looked to be 11 or 12 at her side. I welcomed the woman and chatted with her. I asked her where she was from and said her daughters were lovely. She replied, "Thank you! I'm a foster mom and we have adopted quite a few children out of foster care."

I froze because when she said the words "foster mom," I felt heat flow through my body from the top of my head to the soles of my feet. Like a rushing waterfall, the presence of God fell upon me suddenly. I knew instantly that I was standing in a *kairos* moment. *Kairos* is a Greek word that is used to indicate a divinely appointed moment or space of time[1]. Just as I was completely convinced that Scott would be a father to a generation of fatherless sons, I was just as sure that this woman was sent by the Lord to tell me about foster care.

"Ma'am, are you a believer?" I asked.

"Yes, I am!" She said joyously.

---

[1]   Strong, James. The New Strongs Exhaustive Concordance of the Bible: With Main Concordance, Appendix to the Main Concordance, Topical Index to the Bible, Dictionary of the Greek Testament. Nashville: T. Nelson, 1990, 125.

"I feel the presence of God all over me right now," I said with tears in my eyes. "I believe God sent you to me to tell me about foster care."

She began to share her story, and as she spoke my heart felt as though it would burst. I knew deep inside me that God was pulling me toward foster care. I could hardly wait to run home and talk to Scott about it. I just *knew* that he would feel the same sense of urgency, that same burning that I had felt. How wrong I was.

"Foster care?" Scott said incredulously. "Don't the kids leave? I can't do that, Harmony. I've already lost my ability to have kids naturally. It would kill me to have a child and then have them taken from us. I don't want to do that."

I was stunned. I looked at Scott fiercely. "God told me you are called to be a father to a generation of fatherless sons. The sons are in foster care! I know it! God wouldn't lead us down this path to break our hearts. Sure, some of the children might return, but we will also have the opportunity to adopt."

"How do you know?" Scott was angry. He was not up for more heartache. He found my faith insidious, a slap in the face after all he had been through in his life. How could I expect him to believe that God would be faithful to give us forever children?

"I just know! I believe what God told me about you. You can't stop God's Word from coming to pass. He will accomplish it even though you doubt Him."

"Harmony, God clearly doesn't want me to be a dad. Almost every man is guaranteed to father children. I don't even have that going for me."

"That's nonsense," I scoffed. "Scott, you know I'm adopted by my dad. Dan Ramsey didn't have to be my dad. He *chose* me. God wants us to rescue orphans. Anyone can make a baby. Not everyone can heal a wounded child. That is your job."

LEAPING IN FAITH

I set my face like flint that day, and it has been set every day since then. Over the last seven years, I have watched the Father transform our lives. Along the way God has asked us to take important steps of obedience. These steps felt costly at the time, but were nothing in comparison to the blessings that the Father had prepared to pour out on us. He asked me to quit my job in timeshare and go back to school to become a music teacher. By God's grace, we obeyed and Scott supported me through my schooling. He asked us to sell our home in Wisconsin and move across the country to Oregon. Scott had never lived outside of the state, but by God's grace, we obeyed. God asked Scott to give up hundreds of acres of beautiful and productive hunting and fishing land owned by his family. And though it was excruciating, God gave Scott the courage to leave it behind. The Father asked us to move 2,600 miles away from our families. Even though it was painful, God placed the thrill of adventure in our hearts and gave us the courage to replant ourselves. He asked me to take a job that was not ideal, and God gave us the grace to obey. The Lord asked us to attend a church where loving community and accountability encouraged healing and growth. Even though we have been pruned and corrected, by God's mercy, we have obeyed. And through this process of obedience, transition, pruning and growth, I continued to believe the prophetic word that I had released over Scott's life three days after meeting him.

The Father was preparing us. He was training us and molding us. He knew exactly what we would need for the work that He had called us to - the same work that He Himself does each day: the job of birthing sons after His own image. Jesus experienced the real cost on the Cross. The cost was death. The Father was calling us to take up our crosses and die to ourselves so that many sons could come into His kingdom. We were dying in little ways. Our loving Father was preparing us for the greatest death of all: to love those who do not love you until the love given transforms the one who is loved.

HEAR THEIR VOICES

Within these pages you may experience what I experienced that day in the foyer of a timeshare resort. God is calling you to a generation of orphans. Indeed, He is calling all of us in some capacity to minister to the least, the lost, the forgotten. No one is exempt from the commandment given us in James 1:27:

> *Pure and undefiled religion before God and the Father is this: to visit orphans and widows in their trouble, and to keep oneself unspotted from the world. (NKJV)*

We must not excuse ourselves from the words of John:

> *By this we know love, because He laid down His life for us. And we also ought to lay down our lives for the brethren. But whoever has this world's goods, and sees his brother in need, and shuts up his heart from him, how does the love of God abide in him? My little children, let us not love in word or in tongue, but in deed and in truth.*
>
> *1 John 3:16-18 (NKJV)*

In fact, I dare you. I dare you to read this book with an open heart and a listening mind. I dare you not to set up barriers in your emotions that would hinder your heart from being broken. I dare you to look into the eyes of a child who has been abused and abandoned by the ones that should have loved him or her. I dare you to look and not look away until that child's brokenness becomes your burden. I dare you to let the conviction cut deep like a knife until the words spill out of your soul, "Lord, what must I do?" Brothers and sisters, I ask you to hear the cry. Because a cry is rising from the young people of our nation and from the nations of the earth.

See us.
We are not invisible.
Hold us.
We are longing to be cradled.
Choose us.
Just as God has chosen you.
Love us.
Plumb our capacity to love you back.
Clothe us.
Drive out the cold dark.
Speak of us -
Until the whole world is listening.

We will go on a journey together through the pages of this book. This is more than our story. This is not merely a memoir of one family's ministry to children. This is a wake-up call to the Body of Christ. This is the sound of a trumpet that Scott and I pray will shake a sleeping giant. Can you feel the shaking? Something deep within you is stirring. That thing is our collective power to change the world.

CHAPTER 1

Where is The Church

If My people who are called by My name will humble themselves, and pray and seek My face, and turn from their wicked ways, then I will hear from heaven, and will forgive their sin and heal their land.

II Chronicles 7:14 (NKJV)

The evangelical denominations have been catalyzed in the last few years. This catalyzing centers around the issue of abortion. A person just has to venture onto the social media platforms to hear the strongly word opinions of church leaders about the murder of unborn children. There are a million memes that have been created to advocate for the little lives in the womb, and every prayer warrior is sharing them. Recently, New York codified the rulings of Roe v. Wade in their laws. The Reproductive Healthcare Act removed the penalties for injuring an unborn child, and it made abortion legal until birth with approval from a doctor. The church's outrage was unanimous, and rightly so. The outrage that this stirred lead to a powerful State of the Union address given by the President of the United States.

"Lawmakers in New York cheered with delight upon the passage of legislation that would allow a baby to be ripped from the mother's womb moments before birth.

These are living, feeling, beautiful babies who will never get the chance to share their love and dreams with the world…Let us work together to build a culture that cherishes innocent life, and let us reaffirm a fundamental truth: All children — born and unborn — are made in the holy image of God."[1]

Well done, Mr. President, the church as a whole cried. They loudly applauded his support of the "Born Alive Act" and they seemed to love him even more than they did the day before. I, too, was greatly moved by his comments and agree wholeheartedly that abortion is abhorrent and demonic. I stand with Solomon who called the hands that shed the blood of the innocent an abomination to the Lord (Proverbs 6:16-18). I was grateful that the President of the United States stood before the joint Congress and pleaded for the lives of the innocent.

As his words were still hanging in the air over the chamber, however, I could hear the quiet voice of Holy Spirit communicating with my spirit. "What about those who are already born? What of those whose innocence is being stolen by the family who was meant to protect them? What of those who society has deemed 'unadoptable'? Teenage boys who have already committed crimes that make them unattractive to clean little families in white-washed suburbia - what of them? Does anyone mourn over the loss of their potential? Where is the outrage? Where are the million marchers for a child who has lived in six different foster homes within two years?"

My point here is not to imply we should back down from our fight against abortion. Abortion is a great evil and should be rooted out of our society. I would argue, however, that the issues in our society go back to the *main* issue, which is the systematic destruction of the family unit.

---

[1]   Trump, Donald J. "State Of The Union Address." Address, State Of The Union, United States Congress, Washington, D.C., February 5, 2019.

GOD'S ORIGINAL INTENTION

Then God said, "Let us make man in Our image, according to Our likeness; let them have dominion over the fish of the sea, over the birds of the air, and over the cattle, over all the earth and over every creeping thing that creeps on the earth." So God created man in His own image; in the image of God He created him; male and female He created them. Then God blessed them, and God said to them, "Be fruitful and multiply; fill the earth and subdue it; have dominion over the fish of the sea, over the birds of the air, and over every living thing that moves on the earth."

Genesis 1:26-28 (NKJV)

When God created humans, He intended for them to be a mirror image of His nature and character, and relationship is intrinsically part of who God is. It is a beautiful and important aspect of our God that He lives in community. The Father, the Son and the Holy Spirit are a family whose members live in perfect unity, serving, supporting and loving one another eternally. In the first chapter of Genesis, God confirms that in order for man to demonstrate the image of the unseen God, he must be set within a family unit. "Let us create man in *Our* (emphasis added) image, according to *Our* likeness; let *them* have dominion… Be fruitful and multiply…" In this passage, the Trinity communicates His desire for His children to live in unity with one another and to create families that will steward each other and the earth.

When I read chapter one of Genesis, I am blessed by God's declaration over His creation. On each day, the Trinity creates something that has never been seen before, important aspects of the earth that would make it the perfect habitat for man. With each passing day of creation, God proclaims that what He has created is good. In my imagination, I see God striding among the trees He spoke. I see the animals approach Him and He lays a great hand on the head of buffalo. He says, "You are good, dear one." The animals leap with joy at God's holy presence. On the sixth day, God stoops down and digs His mighty fingers into the soft dirt. He begins to fashion a man from the clay in His hands. When He has molded the man to look just like his Father God, the Trinity lays His loving hands on the shoulders of the man and breathes into him. They are face-to-face as God breathes, and when Adam opens his eyes for the first time, he is looking into the eyes of his Father. What a beautiful and intimate moment that is. God looks into Adam's eyes and says, "You are very good, son."

Soon after this powerful scene, however, we have a moment where God identifies an aspect in the setting that is not good. After God has spent an entire chapter of His Word explaining how very good His creation is, it is almost surprising to hear Him say the words, "It is not good." Where does the Trinity use this description? He calls man's *aloneness* not good. The Trinity, the Holy God who is also a Heavenly Family, recognizes that in order for man to perfectly reflect the nature and character of his Heavenly Father, he must live in relationship to someone who is his equal and helper. He must be one with another who is his perfect counterpoint in order to truly be like God.

Paul affirms to the New Testament believers the divine mystery that is marriage. Ephesians chapter five tells us that the marriage of a husband and wife is to reflect the relationship that Christ has with His bride, the church. This is a reinstatement of that beautiful union that Adam and Eve had in the Garden of Eden. Together, that first couple showed all of creation just what the Heavenly Family - Father, Son and Holy Spirit - was really like. Jesus came to restore all aspects of our reflective nature. We can now demonstrate to the world what God's unity looks like by living in union with our spouse. In fact, there is no more important work to do on the earth than the work we do to love our spouse. It is our first stewardship and ministry. We will discuss this more in chapter four.

Paul also confirms our call to a greater community in 1 Corinthians 12. He describes all believers as a body, with many different parts functioning uniquely. Paul tells us it would be ridiculous for every believer to be an eye, because we would be missing the gift of smelling under those circumstances. He calls us to live in unity, allowing each member to contribute to the health and success of the whole body. He instructs us to rejoices when others rejoice and weep when others are sorrowful. He reiterates our role as God's mirror to the world. In the book of Psalms, David paints for us a beautiful picture of God's nature reflected in His children. Psalm 133 says, "Behold, how good and how pleasant it is for brethren to dwell together in unity! It is like the precious oil upon the head, running down on the beard, the beard of Aaron, running down the edge of his garments... For there the Lord commanded the blessing - life forevermore." Where do we experience life abundant and eternal? Where do we experience the commanded blessing of the Lord? It is when we live within community, reflecting God's heart of unity.

In contrast to God's love of unity, God uses strong language to describe His feelings about division. In Proverbs chapter five, God commands husbands to be faithful to their wives and to enjoy them always. He desires that husbands and wives would drink deeply of each other's love and to keep their eyes fixed on the covenant they have made with their spouse. He warns young people against the fruit of promiscuity, namely death. Throughout the book of Proverbs, God encourages the family unit, asking children to obey the commands of their fathers and the law of their mothers. He instructs fathers to discipline their children so that they will grow up with a love for God's word.

Malachi tells us that God hates divorce. He rebukes the Levites, who have abandoned their wives to be unfaithful with foreign women. Jesus reiterates God's heart toward marriage in the Sermon on the Mount. Jesus tells his disciples that marriage is sacred in God's eyes and that He intended that husband and wife would become one flesh. God has created the union between husband and wife to reflect His own heavenly community, and divorce is a demonic force that drives people away from their primary calling.

DO NOT BE IGNORANT

If God feels so strongly about the family, if he has called the family to reflect His person so that the world can see who He is, it is no surprise that Satan's strategy is to destroy families. The very first sin drove a wedge between Eve and her husband. Adam blamed God and the woman for his behavior, instead of owning his responsibility as the steward of the garden. The woman blamed the snake. Satan had deceived Eve. He called into question her authority to reflect God's nature and character. He introduced doubt into Eve's mind, by saying that God was holding back from Eve some aspect of His nature. She forgot that she and Adam were the mirror into which God gazed. She allowed lies to separate her from her identity. Eve abandoned her union with God, and she was cursed with relationship problems:

To the woman He said: "I will greatly multiply your sorrow and your conception; in pain you shall bring forth children; Your desire shall be for your husband, and he shall rule over you. Then to Adam He said, "Because you have heeded the voice of your wife, and have eaten from the tree of which I commanded you, saying, 'You shall not eat of it': Cursed is the ground for your sake; in toil you shall eat of it all the days of your life. Both thorns and this-

*tles it shall bring forth for you, and you shall eat the herb
of the field. In the sweat of your face you shall eat bread till
you return to the ground, for out of it you were taken; for
dust you are, and to dust you shall return."*

Genesis 3:16-19 (NKJV)

Let us look at the verse closely for a moment. God said, because of your choice, Eve, experiencing the blessings of motherhood will be excruciatingly painful for you. You were created to bring new life into the earth, just as I speak and new life appears. I breathe and galaxies are formed. Birthing should be as easy as breathing for you. Instead it will be the most painful experience of your life. You no longer will come directly to me for your identity. Before sin, you gazed into my eyes. I held your attention with my love. Now, you will gaze somewhere else, and what you will see will not fill you as I do. You will seek fulfillment in your marriage, and instead of stewarding you and loving you, your husband will subjugate you. No longer will you experience beautiful equality and mutual servanthood. You will fight to regain the position of effortless authority that I created for you in the garden.

In Adam's case, the curse God speaks can be summed up in three words: obsession with work. Before sin, Adam was a partner with God, naming the animals. He lived in loving relationship with his wife. He had no need to strive in order to feed himself or his family, because the garden was full of good fruit to eat. Adam had time and desire to focus on his relationships with God and his wife. There was an ease to everything that Adam and Eve did in the garden because of their connection with God. They were living in the sabbath rest of the Lord. Sin took Adam out of rest and into striving.

Since that time, it has been Satan's main concern to destroy the unity and love that was given to that first family unit in the garden of Eden. God honored Abel's sacrifice but reject-

15

ed Cain's offering. Cain murdered his brother Abel because of jealousy. Abram saw nothing wrong with being intimate with Sarah's handmaid in order to have a son (even though God had spoken from heaven and told Abram his family line would come through Sarah). Sarah loathed her handmaid, who had become arrogant after the birth of her son. Sarah demanded that Abram send the woman and her son out into the desert because of jealousy. Jacob willfully deceived his father because he jealously coveted the first-born blessing that should have gone to his older brother Esau. The sons of Jacob sold Joseph to Ishmaelite slave traders because of - wait for it - *jealousy*. They longed to be important in the eyes of their father, and they saw their younger brother as threat to their individual positions in their father's house.

Where were the fathers in all of these circumstances? Adam was silent in the face of his sons' rivalry. He was not even mentioned in the story. That seems curious in a time and culture where men ruled over their households. What was Abram's response to Sarah's jealousy? Did he defend and protect his son Ishmael? We can read for ourselves that Abram was the one who sent Hagar and Ishmael away. Can you imagine being the boy in the story?

Father, why are you sending me away? I love you. What have I done? Why are you rejecting me?

Through the child's eyes, we can see just what a cruel taskmaster jealousy can be. We can see how a missing father can completely destroy the identity of a son. Abram's choice to reject his oldest son caused conflict in a family that has lasted thousands of years. We still see this conflict between the Jewish and Arab peoples in the Middle East today. If we look at the Muslim people as a whole and the Jewish people as a whole, we can see that they are really two brothers who both long to be their father's favorite. Ishmael is desperate to be embraced. He does not understand why he is being rejected. *I am Abram's son, too!* Tell me, where are the fathers?

Jealousy is the cry of a human heart *to be seen by and important to someone.* When we see that something or some-one has supplanted us in the heart of the one we love, it causes strong emotions of anger, rejection and bitterness. If we only look at the book of Genesis, we will find example after exam-ple where the family unit was torn apart at its seams by mem-bers who were longing for the identity that only union with God and unity with others could bring them. They hungered to reflect God's nature and character, as they were created to do. Instead of returning to the Image-Giver, however, they perpetuated the curses spoken over them. Women turned to their husbands to find fulfillment and were often disappointed (think of Tamar). Instead of giving relationships the position importance they were meant to have, men turned to their work to find out who they were. The children looked to the fathers to find their identity, and instead found rejection and abandon-ment. They found fathers who were too focused on their own missing identities to tell their children who they were meant to be.

THE ORPHAN SPIRIT

The orphan spirit is a plague that has been spreading since the dawn of time. The orphan spirit is a direct product of the separation from God we experienced because of Adam and Eve's sin. In some way we all face the orphan spirit. We all long to know who our father is. For some of us this desire is exacerbated by a missing earthly father. The man who was called to show us the nature and character of our Heavenly Father, who could have led us back to a face-to-face intimacy with our Heavenly Father, has failed us. In some of our lives, he failed by sowing his fear and anger in our hearts. He failed by taking out on us his own lack of identity. Some of us have been abused by our fathers, beaten or molested by the one who was called to protect us. In other cases, our fathers were missing all together. These failed fathers are passing on the orphan spirit to their children.

There are powerful signs that a person is suffering under an orphan spirit. The evidence usually lies in the persons words. Our words are a picture of our thought life and reflect our inner meditations. In other words, these people will show you their hearts by their words.

> *"Either make the tree good and its fruit good, or else make the tree bad and its fruit bad; for a tree is known by its fruit. Brood of vipers! How can you, being evil, speak good things? For out of the abundance of the heart the mouth speaks. A good man out of the good treasure of his heart brings forth good things, and an evil man out of the evil treasure brings forth evil things. But I say to you that for every idle word men may speak, they will give account of it in the day of judgment. For by your words you will be justified, and by your words you will be condemned."*
>
> *Matthew 12:33-37 (NKJV)*

These people say things like, "I hate myself", "My life is meaningless", or "I don't have any talents". Some of these people may not say these things, but their behaviors demonstrate their lack of purpose and direction. These are the same people who say, "I'm looking out for number one" and "Nobody tells me what to do". They have little respect for people and institutions with authority. They may have difficult relationships at work and they may disregard laws. The orphan spirit can also manifest as independence. When I hear a person say, "I don't need to go to church. I can talk to God in my backyard," or "I don't need anyone to tell me who God is," I know that person is suffering from an orphan spirit. I choose not to stand in judgment of these people because I too have walked this road, as most of us have.

When I was five months old, my mother, Michele, left my abusive and unfaithful biological father. She took my older sister and me to live with our grandparents. I spent the first four years of my life in the safety and love that my mother and grandparents provided. They taught me about Jesus, they taught me to pray and study God's Word, and they prophesied over my life consistently. During this time, my mother met and remarried the man who would choose to become my father. Dan Ramsey was willing to step in where another man had failed. He loved me unconditionally.

Fathering me was not always an easy job. Even though I had only spent five months in my biological father's home, and I had been blessed to be in a Spirit-filled family with my mother and grandparents, it seemed that damage had already been done to my identity by the choices of my earthly dad. He had passed on to me an orphan spirit, an identity missing a foundation that can only come from the Image-Giver. As he had never known the love of God, nor the love of a human father, he had never been instructed or trained in fatherhood. It makes sense that he was incapable of fathering, as he had never been fathered himself. Emotionally, I reflected the brokenness of my biological father. I needed someone to lead me back to Eden, back to a face-to-face encounter with my Heavenly Father.

On the other hand, the man who stepped up to be my father, Dan Ramsey, had the experience of a father and mother who invested in him. My father's biological mother had personal struggles that left her young children vulnerable. My grandfather and his second wife rescued my dad and uncle from a desperate situation, and their stepmother chose to adopt them as her own children. My grandfather and grandmother demonstrated God's fathering heart to my dad. As a young adult, my father was then introduced to his Heavenly

Father and became a member of God's eternal family. How was he able to show up consistently, supporting and loving me through self-hatred, fear and rebellion? His father, my grandfather, had given him a glimpse of the nature and character of God. When he met the Image-Giver, his Heavenly Father, my dad was ready to exchange the orphan spirit for the spirit of a son. He chose to lead me in this same pattern, even when I resisted his love and correction. Just as my grandmother had adopted him, my dad Dan made an important decision to adopt my older sister and me. He gave us his last name, just as God the Father gives us His name. He passed on to us a sense of belonging. He stirred up in us a deeper understanding that we are God's daughters, even when human beings fail us. He was more than a natural father - he was and is our spiritual father.

THE SUPERNATURAL FAMILY

When Jesus came, he offered humankind a massive redo of the Garden of Eden. The Son of God came on the scene, full of the Holy Spirit and power, to restore our authority to reflect God's image. Jesus became the prototype that each son and daughter was to be patterned after. He gives us back the power to reflect God's beautiful familial nature. In the desert, Jesus was tempted in similar ways to that first disastrous temptation - would Jesus choose to exalt Himself, or would He choose to stay submitted to His intimate relationship with the Father? Unlike the first Adam and his wife, the last Adam chose to reflect the Father's image perfectly. Jesus chose to believe God's Word instead of grasping for a cheap imitation. You see, what Satan offered Eve was a farce, a sham. He told Eve, if you eat of this tree you will be like God, and He does not want that for you! Similarly, our enemy told Jesus, if you bow down to me, I will make you king of all the nations of the earth (Luke 4:6-7). Wait. Did the Trinity give man and woman His image in Genesis or not? Was Jesus not already King of kings and Lord of lords? Jesus believed what Eve rejected. That all authority had already been given to the Son. He was not fooled Satan's divisive words, and neither should you be.

Jesus not only believed what God said about Him. He also believed that He was called to prophesy identity over every person He came in contact with. He released His own nature and character to those around Him. Although Jesus was never married and had no natural children, Jesus was a Father to his disciples, men and women who followed Him and loved Him. There is no better picture of this than the picture Jesus paints of Himself as the Good Shepherd.

I alone am the Good Shepherd, and I know those whose hearts are mine, for they recognize me and know me, just as my Father knows my heart and I know my Father's heart. I am ready to give my life for the sheep. And I have other sheep that I will gather which are not of this Jewish flock. And I, their shepherd, must lead them too, and they will follow me and listen to my voice. And I will join them all into one flock with one shepherd.

John 10:14-16 (The Passion Translation)

Jesus is describing for His believers His sacrificial love for them. There is no more powerful example of a father's heart than a leader who is willing to sacrifice his life for his charges. This kind of leadership can be demonstrated, not only by natural fathers, but by those who are called to lead spiritually. Jesus taught us that a true leader serves. The most powerful person is not the one who lords his power over others, but the one who puts others before himself.

In a day when we have a generation of missing fathers, we cannot assume that the children of our communities are experiencing this servant leadership at home. According the U.S. Census Bureau (found on Fatherhood.org), 19.7 million children live without a father in their homes. This is devastating to the development of each child who experiences it. Fatherhood. org has coined the term "the father factor", a phrase to indicate the impact that fatherlessness has on a child. The statistics are staggering. Children from fatherless homes are four times more likely to live in poverty and two times more likely to experience childhood obesity. Children without fathers are more likely to commit crimes and go to jail, and girls without fathers are seven times more likely to experience teen pregnancy. Our children need an intervention. They need fathers to arise from unlikely places.

Where natural families have failed this generation of children, God is calling believers to create supernatural families. Fathers and mothers who are filled with the Spirit of Holiness, just as Jesus was, are called to reflect God's familial nature. They are called to create families that redefine the word, just as Jesus did.

While Jesus was still speaking to the crowds, his mother and brothers came and stood outside, asking for him to come out and speak with them. Then someone said, "Look, your mother and brothers are standing outside, wanting to have a word with you." But Jesus just looked at him and said, "Let me introduce you to my true mother and brothers." Then gesturing to the disciples gathered around him, he said, "Look closely, for this is my true family. When you obey my heavenly Father, that makes you a part of my true family."

Matthew 12:46-48 TPT

Jesus was not implying that his mother and brothers had no value to Him. If that were true, He would not have turned to John while he hung on the cross and committed His mother into John's care. Jesus was saying that He was taking the definition of family back to its roots - in the image of His Father. Anyone who imitates the Father is part of God's family.

Lately there has been a huge push by our society to open the boundaries of the definition of family. Because of this pressure, the church has become a much friendlier environment for families that are outside of the traditional standards. We have become more accepting of interracial marriages, for example, which were illegal at one point in our nation's history. Long after those laws were removed, the church finally began changing its attitude. Many would agree that these changes are good. The church should not be a place where white supremacy can hide and be protected. In the 70's and 80's, the church began acknowledge and embrace single moms. Before that time, having a child out of wedlock was considered a great shame and could destroy a young woman's standing in her community. The church should be helping young single mothers to succeed so that girls who find themselves pregnant are less tempted to have an abortion. If we embrace and sustain them, they will no longer have to hide in the shadows.

The problem with the scenario is that society is always ahead of the church in defining freedom and the church seems to be playing catch-up. Women went back to work in the 70's, while some churches were still refusing to allow women to wear pants. Four decades later, we have seen an uptick in female pastors and ministers. Mothers in the church, such as Joyce Meyers and Beth Moore, have helped to create momentum for a generation of Deborah's to arise. They paved the way through tough resistance so that women of faith can share the Gospel with greater freedom than ever before. Instead of lagging behind the world, we ought be be setting the standard and drawing in the unbelievers with the beauty of our reflection of God's love.

When we follow the world, the world gets to decide what freedom looks like. They get to manipulate truth so that it matches their desires. These desires are driven by an identity-starved agenda. The definition of family has of late been expanded to include homosexual couples and "transgender" people. Because the world was out in front, we find they have already made the decision to change the definition of family to suit their own a world-view with no Image-Giver, a world view where man defines himself. Homosexual and transgender people groups are highly loved and important to our Heavenly Father. They have the same innate need to be defined as each of us does. The problem is, the creation does not get to define itself. That is the right of the Designer, and the Designer is God.

It is time for the Body of Christ to tap into God's thoughts concerning the family and to bring His mind onto the world stage. His thoughts on this matter are not a secret - He has revealed them in His Word and through the person of His Son. We are called to invade the world with His Kingdom, not to sit idly by and allow the world to make its own decisions. Jesus is the conquering King! We are His heirs, the princes and princesses of the Kingdom of God, and we are called to shift the culture we live in. We must recognize that we enter every environment from a position of victory and authority. We are only enforcing what God has already established in the Heavenly Realms. What does that mean for the family? It means, the family begins to look like Heaven.

In Heaven, there is the Father sitting on a Throne. At His right hand sits the Son who is returning for His bride. The Heavenly Realm is the realm of family. Supernatural families are called to reflect the Heavenly Family.

1. Father is the Servant-Leader who is lavishing His love and favor upon each of us eternally.
2. Jesus is a gentle Husband who passionately pursues His bride, the Church, while waiting in peace for a time that only the Father knows. He prays for His bride and cherishes her.

3. The Holy Spirit is the *Dunamis* power of the Father who makes each of us into the image of the Son.
4. The 24 elders, our big brothers and sisters in the faith, stand around the throne laying down their crowns in continual worship of the Lamb's majesty.
5. Around them is the Great Multitude from every nation, each one has been grafted into the tree of God. Each one has been adopted into His family and has been given a new name. Their worship is a sound that cannot be silenced.

Imagine with me what our churches would look like and feel like and sound like if we reflected the Heavenly family. Imagine a home with a father and mother who lavish their love on each other and their children in an eternal way. They shower with affection, are slow to anger and rich and abounding in mercy when their children fail. Imagine a husband who passionately pursues his wife and is consistently present for his children. Imagine a man who prophesies over their lives, releasing the Word of God into their inner being until they become a reflection of that Word. Imagine with me a home where the Holy Spirit has a seat at the table. His presence is cultivated and enjoyed. Imagine older brothers and sisters learning to reflect God's nature and character to their younger siblings. And imagine, if you will, families where the orphan is rescued and grafted in. Imagine boys and girls of all creeds and colors having their pasts redeemed and their futures rewritten because of a divine intervention. Imagine if the Body of Christ took God's model and ran ahead of the world. I believe the lost would run after God's design with all of their might, because they hunger for the same gift we offer a generation of fatherless sons: Identity.

HARMONY KLINGENMEYER

CHAPTER 2

Our Family

In the next pages, we will look closely at what "supernatural family" means for us. In the introduction to this book, we dipped our toe in the story of Scott and Harmony. If you were in a hurry and skipped the introduction, I highly recommend that you go back and read it now. It is the beginning of our love story and it holds insights into the reasons why we became foster parents in the first place. Scott and I are on a journey to discover God's design for the supernatural family. We desire for each child to come face-to-face with their Heavenly Father, as it is in Heaven at this very moment. The story of us is a story of heartbreak and victory, of long nights, long trips, lots of tears and laughter. I want to share our story with you so that you can walk down the path of fostering and adoption before you jump in for yourselves. I want you to understand what it looks like in the real world. It is not a fantasy life. No one who has experienced "the system" would characterize it as such. We all experience it differently, so it will not look exactly the same for your family, if you choose to take the leap. But if you accept this challenge, there are some common themes that run through every foster family's story that will run through yours. Scott and I want to share those themes with you, so that your hearts can be prepared to some degree.

We begin by sharing our personal stories that brought us to a place where our hearts and minds were open to becoming foster parents. God is willing to take each person on a trip that involves personal transformation, and this transformation is what the world needs to encounter in order to come to know Jesus personally. Scott's growing-up years looked very different than mine, and we will discuss how it is extremely important that children are mentored by adults from varying backgrounds and strengths. Just as there are many different types of children who find themselves in "the system," there is a need for many different types of adults to mentor them. We want to confront and dispel the idea that one must be an educator or a scholar or a reverend in order to minister to the needs of a foster child. These children need your presence, not your perfection. They need your consistent and loving boundaries, not your boundless knowledge. They need the example of your humility and repentance, not a person who has never been tested enough to experience failure.

The goal of foster care is not a certain level of success. Each child will bring with them a history of abuse, neglect, pain, diagnoses and prescriptions. Each child will need special interventions, modifications and assistance that are unique to their circumstances. They will bring a mind with a will and a body with personal power, and each one will have decisions to make along the way that will lead them to differing levels of transformation. Have no doubt, you will fail. Do not be afraid, however, you will also see the sun rise on a new and victorious day. This chapter is all about the process of how God opened our eyes to see the need of our society, a need that God has called us to meet. This chapter is about helping each child to discover the eternal love of God so that they can begin loving themselves. It is the work of the Holy Spirit to transform lives. Parents are offered the opportunity to partner with Him in this work, to open the door for His ministry in our homes. Scott and I have not mastered this journey. We are not experts. We are, as all parents are, in the process of growing and maturing in God. We bring to parenting our own trials and struggles. We bring different strengths and weaknesses. The amazing thing about partnering with the Holy Spirit is this: As you allow Him to transform you, He will pour through you to the little lives around you. We invite you into the process with us. We invite you to let Holy Spirit move in your hearts in a new way, as He has done in us and will continue to do. I reiterate a previous statement here: allow your heart to feel. Let God convict you. Let Him call into question your long-held views and you will be taking the first step toward understanding His deep love for a generation of fatherless children.

THE INSPIRATION

There are seeds lying inside each human that only need a little watering before they will begin to take root and sprout. These seeds are lying dormant in us, like the bones lay sleeping in Ezekiel. In the 37th chapter, God transports Ezekiel to a vast valley full of bones. Some may only see a mass grave, but God sees the framework for a living army. These dry bones wait for God's voice to be released over them. God asks Ezekiel, "Can these bones live?" This is an important question. Better than anyone, God knows the potential He has deposited in every person. The question is not what God knows about the bones, but what Ezekiel believes. God Himself could have spoken over the dry bones and commanded them to live. Yet, He chooses to operate within community, partnering with Ezekiel's voice. He chooses a son as the avenue for His dunamis power.

Again He said to me, "Prophesy to these bones, and say to them, 'O dry bones, hear the word of the Lord! Thus says the Lord God to these bones: "Surely I will cause breath to enter into you, and you shall live. I will put sinews on you and bring flesh upon you, cover you with skin and put breath in you; and you shall live. Then you shall know that I am the Lord."'" So I prophesied as I was commanded;

and as I prophesied, there was a noise, and suddenly a rattling; and the bones came together, bone to bone. Indeed, as I looked, the sinews and the flesh came upon them, and the skin covered them over; but there was no breath in them. Also He said to me, "Prophesy to the breath, prophesy, son of man, and say to the breath, 'Thus says the Lord God: "Come from the four winds, O breath, and breathe on these slain, that they may live."'" So I prophesied as He commanded me, and breath came into them, and they lived, and stood upon their feet, an exceedingly great army.

Ezekiel 37:4-10 (NKJV)

This partnership between God and His children can be seen throughout the entirety of the Scripture and is a key to understanding how God works in us. We are called to recognize what God has placed within us and partner with God to see those seeds cultivated until good fruit is produced in and through our lives. Ezekiel prophesies over the framework in the valley and the dry bones become a great host. Within your family, and indeed within your own life, there are dormant seeds. You may be able to identify them easily—a dream that you have given up on, a marriage that is falling apart, a business idea that has never come to fruition. Some of these seeds, however, you might not even know are within you. Within you lies a framework that God can use to build a great army. It is time to reveal those seeds. It is time to speak prophetically over your seeds. You can be the one who takes an active role in the future of your family by using your voice and choice to cultivate your family's potential.

My father's adoptive mother was an important figure in his life, and even though I never met her, I feel the impact of her legacy. That legacy is adoption. I recognize that she and my grandfather were seed planters and cultivators in our family line. I see the inheritance she and my grandfather chose to lay up for their family. Even as a child, I was always inspired by my father. He is a tenacious man, the sort of person who never gives up and who is not swayed by the everyday roller-coaster of life. He rejects emotionalism, preferring instead to think about things and make a logical decision. He is a dedicated family man who considers the needs of his family as more important than his own. He has always inspired me with his heart of service and his willingness to sacrifice for the good of others. My dad received some of these personality traits from his father and mother; others were lying dormant within him, planted there by his Heavenly Father in past generations. When he returned to the Image-Giver, those seeds came alive within him. My father took an active role in developing his God-given potential. He took the legacy he was given by his father and mother and multiplied it.

My father planted and also prophesied over the framework of God's nature within me. From the very beginning of my life, I was encouraged to recognize and believe what God said about me. My father and I are very different people, but my father did not try to make me into his own image. Instead, he recognized the gifts and callings on my life and encouraged me to *run in my lane*. My dad taught me to reject the changing opinions of my peers and to stand firmly on the truth of God's Word. And he was not the only one who planted and prophesied over my life. My mother, Michele, and my maternal grandparents took an active role, speaking truth over me and cultivating the presence of the Holy Spirit in my life. Just as Ezekiel commanded the breath of life to blow upon the dry bones, my father, mother and grandparents opened the door for God's presence to dominate my young life. The seeds were never really dormant in me because my family would not allow what God had placed in me to go to waste.

When I was 14 years old, my dad approached me and my older sister, Karina, and asked if we would like to be adopted. My first response was, of course! He was the only father

31

I had ever known, but it was more than that. Dan Ramsey was the only man who had ever *fathered me*. I recognized, even at that young age, that fathering is about what you do in a child's life. I knew that a father is present. A father teaches you to ride a bike and tie your shoes, and he shows up for birthday parties and t-ball games. A father is the man who takes you to church and prays over you at night. In my life, that man was Dan Ramsey and no other. I already used his last name even though it was not the name on my birth certificate. The adoption process would entail asking my biological father to relinquish his parental rights, which meant I would have to speak to him on the phone and tell him I wanted to be adopted. I remember that conversation so clearly. My mother sat next to me as I spoke with a stranger on the phone. At one point in the conversation, I remember saying, "Dan Ramsey is my dad."

The stranger replied, "No, he's not. I'm your dad."

I was appalled that he could be so arrogant. I knew instinctively that no man can be a father apart from what that man *does*. I responded, "You need to know that even if you refuse to give up your rights, Dan Ramsey will always be my father." That was the end of the conversation. How did I know what a father was supposed to look like? How did I have the courage to tell the stranger he did not qualify? It was because of the seeds that had been cultivated in my own life. It was because others had *shown me* through their voice and choice what our Heavenly Father looks like.

In contrast to my story of adoption, Scott was raised by his biological father and mother. He grew up in rural Wisconsin, hunting and fishing and living off the land. Scott's father, Butch, passed on to him many important life lessons. He passed on to Scott financial wisdom, which meant that Scott was able to purchase a home at 20 years old. He taught Scott about the plants and animals of the northern forests and how to steward the land well. Butch was a generous man who blessed others financially. He passed on this generosity to his son.

Scott has always fed the poor and helped those less fortunate than himself. He learned this behavior from watching his father. Unfortunately, Butch was not able to teach Scott about God's love, nor was he able to speak identity over Scott. Butch was abused as a boy and carried the pain of his experiences into his adult life. He grew up in an environment where cruel words were the norm and he chose to pass that on to his son, Scott. Scott's mother, Kay, was a loving presence in Scott's life. Even though she took her son to church and showed him consistent love, her presence was not enough to override the voice of a father who lacked identity. Instead of sending a firm message that Scott was worthy and loved, Butch sent mixed messages about Scott's value. He would tell Scott he loved him in one sentence and call him stupid in the next. Butch did this, not because he wanted to hurt Scott, but because Butch believed himself to be worthless and weak. Along with a love for the land and a firm grasp of fiscal responsibility, Butch passed on his own lack of identity to his son.

When Scott and I met, he had no idea of his inner strength. His eyes were blind to the dormant seeds that lay within him. He had spent his life agreeing with the lie that God did not love him. Scott believed God had taken away his ability to father because his life was a mistake. That belief sprang from the way he was treated by his father Butch. When our fathers treat us as if we have no value, we tend to believe them. We tend to equate their ideas with God's ideas, because in the original design, fathers were called to show their children the nature and character of their Heavenly Father. The children still cry out for this image, but the fathers have forgotten to reflect. Instead they pass on their own broken, distorted image. Instead of leaving the seeds asleep, however, God sent the eyes of the Spirit into Scott's life. The potential within Scott to change a generation was so great, God could not allow Scott's life to go to waste. Where did that potential come from? God Himself had planted it there.

33

Scott's story reminds me of another man called to change a generation. That man was John the Baptist. 400 years before Elizabeth and Zechariah came on the scene, a prophet by the name of Malachi spoke these words:

Behold, I will send you Elijah the prophet
Before the coming of the great and dreadful day of the
Lord.
And he will turn
The hearts of the fathers to the children,
And the hearts of the children to their fathers,
Lest I come and strike the earth with a curse.

Malachi 4:5-6 (NKJV)

Can you imagine the excitement of those who first heard the prophecy? What joy it would have struck in the hearts of the lovers of God in that generation. *Elijah is coming! He will cause the fathers to arise and lead this generation back to God!* Little did they know that it would be 400 years until the fulfillment of that prophetic word. I am convinced that many a family has experienced just this sort of situation. Waiting on the fulfillment of God's promises can be discouraging at times. It is easy to lose heart if you have been waiting on your children to come back to God. It can be hard if you have been praying for the salvation of a spouse and they are yet resisting the Holy Spirit. I share Scott's story as a source of encouragement for those who are still waiting. Hidden in Scott were the dry bones of many generations past. In him were all the prophetic words spoken over his family, generation to generation. God was waiting for the perfect time to release those seeds, to breathe upon those bones. And God chose to release those seeds by partnering with his daughter. He used my voice to call out to those dry bones, "Come alive!" Scott's eyes have slowly been opened to God's purposes, even in his weaknesses. If it were not for Klinefelter Syndrome, Scott may never have found himself in a position to father a generation. What the enemy of our souls tried to use to curb Scott's potential became the doorway for God's great victory. Scott and I are a reflection of the prophetic voices that have unlocked our dry bones. Our work as foster and adoptive parents spring from those seeds that others saw and called forth.

THE CALL

As a music teacher, it is my privilege to spend every Monday through Friday passing on the love of music to the children of my community. I have the great privilege of working with a large group of students—more than 700 at two different elementary schools—who spend 60 minutes a week with me. Because I am with the students from kindergarten through fifth grade, I have six years to build relationships with children and to see them grow and develop. I have many opportunities to speak to the seeds I see hidden within them. I get to watch them discover they are capable and brave. It is also the reality of my job that I am privy to the impact of each student's homelife on their academic and socio-emotional development. It is a joy to see the amazing impact a loving father and mother can have on young minds. I also get to see firsthand the pain it causes a child when their father or mother is in jail or out of the picture because of divorce. I am currently picturing the face of a first-grade girl who comes to my class regularly. Once or twice a month, she asks me if she can start music class in the "safe place." In my classroom, I have a corner with pillows and signs with affirming words on them. There are breathing exercises that the students do when they are in the safe place and then they rejoin their class. I used to ask this student why she needed the safe place. She would reply, "I miss my daddy." I found out from her teacher that her father is in prison and will be for quite some time. The child does not comprehend why she needs to be separated from her father. She knows only that he is no longer with her and that she is not allowed to see him. In her small mind, she may feel that it is her fault she cannot be with her daddy. Psychologists agree that children often believe they are the problem in the relationships they have with adults. When their parents separate, children believe they are the cause, instead of putting the blame where it belongs—the adults.

Each season of my life has prepared me for a season I am yet to walk in. When I became a teacher, I knew that God had called me to nurture and educate the next generation. I had glimpses that my training as a teacher and my experiences in the classroom would prepare me for motherhood. What I did not know was the impact each student would have on my heart. My classroom had become a haven for students who felt lonely, out of place, and/or different. At lunch time, a group of students would find their way to my classroom. They would eat their lunches and we would sing around the piano together. When we were not singing, we would discuss their lives, and I would have moments to speak identity over them. I had opportunities to share glimpses of heaven with them without ever mentioning God. When a student would ask me, "Mrs. Klingenmeyer, why do you believe in me? Why do you have such a high opinion of me?" I would tell them, "It's because of what Jesus has done in my life that I can see others the way He sees me." My students felt safe in my classroom, safe to be themselves in a world that is constantly demanding that each person be defined by external forces or by their own changing inner voice. They have lost their compass because they have walked away from the Image-Giver, the One who has the right to define us. In my classroom, each student was released from the pressure of defining him- or herself. Instead they had God's image stirred up within them.

This powerful connection with my students made saying "goodbye" very difficult. Truly, the hardest part of obeying

God and moving to Oregon was leaving behind my students. Even though they were never my children, I loved them in my heart like I would my own child. This was exquisite preparation for the life to which God was calling me. Little did I know at the time that I would hold a three-month-old baby in my arms and then 24 hours later put them in someone else's arms and never see them again. My experiences as a teacher taught me that it is ok to say goodbye. It is ok to mourn for a child you did not give birth to. It is ok to weep for the one you held only for a short while, just as you would mourn for the one who was with you for years. I learned that it was ok to feel indignant when a child was transferred to another school without anyone informing you. I carried these truths into motherhood, and I hold tight to them when I experience the inevitable heartache that comes with the foster life.

In contrast to my years of educational training and classroom teaching, Scott had very little exposure to children before we became parents. Scott never saw himself as a "baby person," although he loved kids and enjoyed playing with youngsters, secretly wishing that he would get to play with his own one day. He loved being an uncle to his five nieces, but he truly believed that he would never experience fatherhood. Because of this devastating belief, Scott never sought opportunities to be with kids. He was convinced that he had nothing of value to give the next generation, and never looked for opportunities to sow. While we were still living in Wisconsin, God opened the first door for Scott to minister to a young man. This young man loved to fish and hunt and was hungry for a man to encourage and uplift him. This young man had many things in common with Scott, and needed a mentor in his life. Scott saw this middle school boy as someone that he could pass on his knowledge of fishing and hunting to and no more. At the time, he did not recognize that God was prying open the door of Scott's heart. God was helping Scott take a baby step toward mentoring and fathering. And while they were fishing, Scott would encourage this boy to study, to be wise about his relationships, and to save money for the future. He would come home and describe their conversations to me. I would smile and say, "You are really helping that young man to see he can have a good future." I would encourage Scott to continue to sow wisdom whenever he had the opportunity. One day when he had returned from duck hunting with his young charge, I told Scott, "You know, you are a mentor to that boy."

Scott said, "I'm only teaching him how to hunt and fish. That's not very important."

I replied, "To him, the time you sow is very valuable. You make him feel safe and loved. Sometimes, your presence is enough to change a child. He feels special because you make time for him." Scott agreed, and I could tell that his heart was beginning to change. Scott began to believe that he could be a loving presence in the life of a child.

I share Scott's viewpoint, because I believe prophetically that there are men and women reading these pages who share Scott's feelings about themselves. They have been convinced by the words of others and by their own emotions that they are unqualified to minister to the next generation. They see their physical limitations or lack of training as an obstacle to their dreams of taking in the orphans. Look at Scott's life. Look at the life of Abraham or Rahab, and tell me, what made them so special that God chose them for His purposes? I am here to confront the lie that God requires you to have some special human training in order to use you in the life of a child. What they need is not your years of training. That child needs your presence. That broken youngster needs an adult to consistently show up with love and patience. That orphan needs an adult to not run away when that child rejects that adult's love. Are you an adult? Can you show up with love? If you can, then God is ready to use you.

If your perspective limits what God can do in and through you, it is time for you to get a new perspective. You must be willing to admit that you believe a lie about God and yourself. You must confront your fear of not being enough. The truth, is none of us is *enough*. The self-help books have it wrong. We are not enough. Instead, we are called to perfectly mirror the One who is *all-sufficient*. Jesus is enough! When we say God is unable to use us, we are limiting His infinite power. We are making YHWH after our own image, instead of reflecting His perfect image. If this is your belief system, I am speaking directly to you right now. Do not be afraid to set down this book and go look at yourself in the mirror. I invite you to use the prayer I have included for you below. This prayer will help you make an exchange with your Kinsman Redeemer, Jesus the Messiah. He has a legal right to redeem all of who you are and to give you in exchange all of who He is. If you are ready to see Him, yourself and others as He sees you, please repeat after me:

> "Lord Jesus, right now I turn and run to you. Holy Spirit, come and arrest my thinking. Right now, I make an exchange with You, Jesus. I give up my limited thinking and receive Your unlimited perspective. I exchange my broken image for Your perfect image. I declare that I believe what You say about me. I agree with You, Kinsman Redeemer, that You have called me to partner with You. I believe that you equip the called and I declare that I lack nothing as I rest in Your perfect love. In Jesus' Name, Amen."

THE WAIT

Scott and I were married four and one-half years before we became parents. He was 36 and I was 32 when Brenden came to live with us. Scott found out at the age of 17 that he would not be able to father children naturally. That means, he waited 19 years to become a father, and it was a long and painful journey for him. I had also waited many years for a loving marriage that might produce children, and when I found out that we would have to come to parenting through unconventional means, I cannot deny that it was emotionally taxing. I believed God would give us children, but I also knew that it would probably be a long process and that it would most likely involve disappointment and heartbreak. The prophetic word that God had given me for Scott planted a deep seed of hope within me that became a beacon of light in our darkest times.

Even though I was convinced that God had called us to foster and adoption, I do not pretend that we did not desire to have children naturally. When God first started talking to me about foster care, Scott was not sure that he could bare the pain of having a child returned to their natural families after they had lived with us. In essence, he believed it would be worse to lose a child that we had loved than to never have loved that child in the first place. I strongly disagreed with him. I knew that in order to have the opportunity to adopt, we would have to take the risk of losing a child. I have always been a risk-taker and an adventurous personality, but I knew it would take an act of God to change Scott's mind. I had already experienced this kind of loss each year as an educator and my heart was prepared to love children, even if it was only temporary. Scott, on the other hand, did not have the blessing of working with children every day. He did not have that immensely fulfilling career to fall back on. He dreaded change in all its forms. The risk of losing a child was the scariest of all.

Because both of us deeply desired to be parents, we decided to try artificial insemination as an option for natural birth. This type of fertility treatment is costly, but not as extreme in price as In Vitro Fertilization. Anyone who has gone through fertility treatments will tell you that it is an expensive and emotionally exhausting experience. We chose a donor and tried three different times to become pregnant. The treatments were nerve wracking and unsuccessful. With each failed treatment, I was left with the feeling that there was something wrong with me. The doctors ran all the available tests and informed me that I was perfectly healthy, and they had no idea why the treatments did not succeed. Having only completed three treatments, I had had enough. The anxiety of waiting and the pain of hoping that led to inevitable feelings of insecurity and failure were too much for me. After this experience, I informed Scott that I was not interested in having kids naturally. I was convinced God was taking us in a different direction and I asked him to pray about filling out paperwork to become foster parents.

I spent many long hours of our lives trying to convince Scott that foster care was the right choice for us. I had not yet learned that it is better to let God do the talking if the goal is heart change. And my timing was off. I was in a hurry because much of my self-esteem was wrapped up in childbearing. I was driven to become a mother because I believed a lie - that my worth as a woman had something to do with how many children I produced. I had forgotten that my worth comes from my God-given position as His image bearer. In essence, I was believing the same lie that Eve believed in the Garden of Eden—we must *do something* to become like God. No human effort can recreate what God alone can do and no human blunder can undo what God has ordained. His Word is forever, and our position in God is eternal. It was never my job to contrive to make God's promises come to pass. But in my thinking, there was a twist. I had replaced partnership with idolatry. Often, we get ahead of God. We have our ideas about how we should make God's promises come to pass. This is not partnership - this attitude is arrogance. My attitude was like that of the Israelites who tried to enter the Promised Land after God had told them they would not be able to conquer the land because of their rebellion and unbelief. Joshua and Caleb had reported that the Promised Land was a good land, flowing with milk and honey, but the ten other spies had been too afraid of the inhabitants of the land to obey God. The Lord struck the ten men with a plague and they died immediately. He also punished the whole camp for listening to their negative report—they would die in the wilderness instead of entering the Promised Land.

When Moses reported the Lord's words to all the Israelites, the people were filled with grief. Then they got up early the next morning and went to the top of the range of hills. "Let's go," they said. "We realize that we have sinned, but now we are ready to enter the land the Lord has promised us." But Moses said, "Why are you now disobeying the Lord's orders to return to the wilderness? It won't work. Do not go up into the land now. You will only be crushed by your enemies because the Lord is not with you. When you face the Amalekites and Canaanites in battle, you will be slaughtered. The Lord will abandon you because you have abandoned the Lord." But the people defiantly pushed ahead toward the hill country, even though neither Moses nor the Ark of the Lord's Covenant left the camp. Then the Amalekites and the Canaanites who lived in those hills came down and attacked them and chased them back as far as Hormah.

Numbers 14:39-45 (NLT)

The men who invaded Canaan without God's permission got ahead of God's timing and left behind His protection and favor. They moved from guaranteed victory to sure defeat. Scott and I experienced this same type of situation when we tried to become foster parents in Wisconsin. We lived in a rural part of the state, and there was very little need for foster parents. When we were denied the opportunity, Scott felt this was a sign that we would never become parents. If I had been patient and waited for God to fulfill His Word, we would not have experienced this added layer of unbelief. God intends for our circumstances to work out for our good and His glory, even when we face the most challenging situations. He enjoys blessing His children and has already ordained our victory.

So we are convinced that every detail of our lives is continually woven together to fit into God's perfect plan of bringing good into our lives, for we are his lovers who have been called to fulfill his designed purpose. For he knew all about us before we were born and he destined us from the beginning to share the likeness of his Son. This means the Son is the oldest among a vast family of brothers and sisters who will become just like him.

Romans 8:28-29 (TPT)

Things get messy when we decide our ideas are better than God's plans. I was in such a hurry to prove my worth by becoming a mother that I inadvertently put my thoughts before God's Word. His plan never included Harmony trying to prove her worth (His image gives me intrinsic worth) and it never included becoming parents before we were prepared for the work (He trains us to succeed). I exalted my own thoughts about God's Word, which is idolatry. He is God and His thoughts are above my thoughts. His ways are above my ways. And the beautiful truth is that His nature does not change, even when we fail. He is capable of using our failures to humble us and discipline our rebellious natures so that His purposes can be accomplished in our lives in spite of our imperfections.

My child, when the Lord God speaks to you,
never take his words lightly,
and never be upset when he corrects you.
For the Father's discipline comes only
from his passionate love and pleasure for you.
Even when it seems like his correction is harsh,

it's still better than any father on earth gives to his child.

Proverbs 3:11-12 (TPT)

During this time we also experienced an unprecedented amount of discomfort in our Wisconsin life. It seemed like there was warfare on all sides. We were newlyweds and we were trying to establish ourselves as a family when we were still defined by our relationships with our parents. We needed to strike out on our own and start listening to God's voice, independent from the many opinions of others. I began to pray that God would give Scott the desire to move away from Wisconsin. This was a huge shift from my previous strategy of lecturing Scott into agreement. I knew that leaving Wisconsin would be especially hard for him, because he had never lived outside of his birth state. In order to leave Wisconsin, Scott would have to exhibit great courage, a willingness to take risks. He would have to sacrifice his hunting land and country living. I knew he would go from being an expert to a novice in all of his favorite hobbies. I have never been prouder of Scott than I was the day he came to me and said, "I think we need to move out of Wisconsin." I knew in that moment that he was listening to the Holy Spirit, not because I had hounded him with my opinions, but because I had stood back and allowed the Father to parent my husband. And my husband had allowed God to change his heart. It was a beautiful partnership. Scott and I have experienced the faithfulness and presence of God in every moment of our story. We have learned that if we will stand still and worship, God will fight on our behalf. He will bring us the victory without the striving and arrogance of human effort.

THE PROMISE KEEPER

In June of 2015, we moved to Oregon. Each step that we took

44

was supernatural. God provided a buyer for our Wisconsin home and an investment that provided us with an excellent down payment for our new house in Oregon. I was offered a job teaching music two hours after my interview and Scott was offered a job within two weeks of us moving into our new home. God led us to a church community that quickly became like a family to us. I started teaching and began to realize we had moved to a town where there was a desperate need for loving adults. Some of the schools in my district experienced more than 70% poverty levels. Children were coming to school hungry and dirty on a regular basis, and there were many opportunities to make reports to Child Protective Services. My heart ached for my students on a daily basis as they began to open up to me about their challenging home lives. God gave me a deep love for the most difficult students, because I knew they had experienced trauma and needed compassion and mercy.

In October 2015, Scott and I revisited the idea of becoming foster parents. We had become aware of the desperate need in our city, and we felt that under the right circumstances, we might be given the opportunity to parent one of my students. We filled out the preliminary paperwork and met with a social worker. We signed up for a mandatory class that would take place in January. And I began to pray. The social worker had informed me that the process of becoming foster parents could take up to a year. We were willing to wait. We had waited this long, and we were not going to rush the process. Then she added this, "It happens sometimes, however, that we need an emergency placement for a child. We look first for adults who know the child, including teachers. If we have an emergency like that, would you be interested?" We both answered emphatically, yes! The Holy Spirit directed me to pray in earnest that a child from my school would need an emergency placement and that the social worker would be put in contact with us.

One day, I was standing in my kitchen cooking. I looked down at the floor because I heard a noise—the sound of laughter. In my spirit, I saw a young boy sitting on my floor building Legos. He had sandy brown hair, but his head was down so that I could not see his face. In my spirit, I knew that the boy was seven years old. I asked the Holy Spirit, "Is this my son?" He replied, "Yes. Pray for him." I began to prophesy over the little boy, commanding the angels to surround him and calling him into our lives. A few days later, I was at a church meeting and one of the pastoral staff approached me. He said, "I don't usually give out prophetic words like this, but I believe God has already spoken to you about this subject and I am supposed to confirm what He spoke. I believed God was going to give you a son, and he will be called a prophet to the nations."

I responded, "I agree. I had a vision of him in my kitchen just three days ago. He is seven years old and will be coming to us soon."

On Wednesday, December 9th, 2015, I was standing outside of the school where I taught, greeting the students as they entered the building. I stood there chatting with an instructional aide who worked with special needs students in our school.

"Do you have any children?" she asked.

"Scott and I want to become foster parents," I replied.

She stared at me in some shock. "Really? I know a student who goes to school here who needs a home right away."

It was my turn to look shocked. "Really?" I said, in amazement.

"I will get permission to share the details with you and come find you at the end of the school day." She hurried away. And then she really did make me wait until the end of the school day. I texted Scott right away. "There's a child here who needs a home. I don't know any details yet, I'll let you know as soon as I hear something." That evening, we spoke with a lady who had been giving this child shelter. She was not the guardian, but she knew the social worker and could get us in contact with her. I did not sleep that night.

In the morning, Child Protective Services came to the school. They asked to speak with me, and I signed paperwork that gave me custody of the child. They brought the child into the office, and there was Brenden, my student. At 11 a,m, in the morning on Thursday, December 10th, 2015, he became my son. He was seven years old and his hair was the sandy brown color of the boy on my kitchen floor.

THE BEGINNING OF US

This was just the beginning of our story as parents. We share it with you, in all of its raw and real glory. We share it for those of you who are waiting on a promise. We know what it feels like to be in the waiting season. We understand the pain of wanting children and wondering when God will fulfill his promises. Now that we stand on the other side of that fulfilled promise, now that we know the joy and heartache that is parenthood, I want to encourage anyone who is married and childless to truly enjoy these days of waiting. Spend time receiving God's love for you. Let His goodness heal the inner hurts and let His presence bring unity between you and your covenant partner. You will never get these days back, and there will be moments in the future where you will look back at them longingly. Parenting is an amazing adventure, but it is also exhausting and painful. Let God continue to grow you and mature you through this season. He will prepare you for what is to come through the circumstances of your present life, and every moment will have been worth it in the future.

Think of what God is planting and developing inside of you at this moment. Perhaps you have been waiting a long time to see the fruit of your labor. Remember that every word you speak is a seed you sow, and the actions you take either water or starve those seeds. When an acorn has been planted in the ground, at first, there is nothing that can be seen with the eyes. On the surface we see only the marred ground where the hole was dug and seed was placed. It might not even look very pretty, because the ground is bare and the dirt is exposed. Yet underneath the ground, water is carrying the nutrients in the dirt into the seed and a small root is growing. It takes time to wait for the little green plant to push pass the surface into the sunlight. All the time it takes, all the little moments where the root goes down and seed cracks open that lead to the moment when we see the little plant sprout are necessary moments of growth and nourishment. And even after that small plant breaks the surface, it will be years before it becomes an oak tree that can bare its own acorns. In the end, however, the fruit will come. If the seed is sown and watered, then the season of rejoicing will inevitably arrive.

If you are blessed with children of your own, but you are wondering if fostering and adopting is right for you and your family, I want to encourage you to think long and hard about the crisis I will present to you in the next chapter. As you read the brutal facts, ask yourself: Who is more qualified or called than the disciple of Jesus to love this fatherless generation? We have all been given the gift of His Holy Spirit, and it is Holy Spirit that will empower you to do what seems impossible. Each of us has something to give the next generation that only we can give. There is a fatherless child in the world right now that is only waiting for the intervention that you can provide. Spiritual sons and daughters are crying out for your obedience, and each of us can experience the blessings that obedience produces in our lives. Consider how God has called you to develop your own supernatural family.

CHAPTER 3

Don't Look Away

There is an insidious epidemic that has swept our nation today, and it exists right underneath our closed eyes. Today, as you are grocery shopping or painting a bedroom or going to work or dropping your kids off at school, there are almost a half million children in foster care in the United States of America.[1] I know, that number is hard to fathom. Nearly 500,000 children are separated from their families at this moment. They have experienced neglect and abuse in varying degrees, and they are afraid and angry. They are living in pain because of what they have experienced, but that pain is secondary to the shock of separation they are feeling because they have been removed from the only life they have ever known. The pain they lived with in the homes of their parents was their normal and not to be questioned. Now that normal is gone, and chaos has arrived. Their worlds have been turned upside down and in their hearts they believe they are to blame for the tragedy they face. Suddenly, there is a police officer and a social worker at their door. They have no idea who these adults are, but they are required to leave with them. They cry and kick and squirm and do not want to leave their homes. But they must. Their parents are angry. They use adult language, and they yell at

---

1   United States. Department of Health and Human Services. The AF-CARS Report. Washington, D.C.: U.S. Dept. of Health and Human Services, Administration for Children and Families, Administration on Children, Youth and Families, Childrens Bureau.

the police officer and call the social worker names. The police officer restrains the children's caregiver as the children watch in horror. The children use the same language as the adults as they are pulled away from their family members and placed in a strange vehicle. Many of them will leave their homes with little to no clothes, blankets or belongings. Some will have no underwear or socks, no toothbrush or coat. Some will leave with bruises and burns and others will carry their wounds internally. Many have not eaten in days.

This is the harsh reality for 500,000 children on any given day in America. In 2017, 690,000 children were served by the foster care system. They are all around us, invisible but very real. Some of this anonymity is necessary to protect the privacy of traumatized children, and HIPAA (Health Insurance Portability and Accountability Act) laws ensure that these children's lives are not on display for all to see. The names and identifying characteristics of children have been changed within this book to ensure no child's right to privacy has been infringed. Can we, however, recognize the struggle of children in our communities and provide solutions that the next generation needs? I want to suggest it is our spiritual and civic duty as Christ-followers and patriots to intervene in these unimaginable circumstances. The first step to solving the crisis our nation faces is to become educated on the subject. In this chapter, we will bring into the harsh light what children are experiencing all around us. I ask you not to look away when it gets ugly. When tears well up in your eyes, keep reading. If you need a break, take it. But remember to come back. Their lives depend on our willingness to destroy the excuses of ignorance and incompetence.

THE COST OF FATHERLESSNESS

In 2017, The most common form of maltreatment that children faced in our country was fatherlessness. 19.7 million

American children lived without a father in 2017[2]. Although most of these children did not experience physical, psychological or sexual abuse, each and every one of them experienced neglect at the hands of their absent fathers. These statistics are not included in the abuse statistics gathered by the federal government, but fatherlessness has a huge impact on the socio-emotional and cognitive development of children. I choose to address fatherlessness first because I believe it is the root cause of child-suffering in our country. The National Fatherhood Initiative has compiled extensive research on the impact of fatherlessness on children, and the cost of a missing father is staggering to our society. We need to recognize that there is a spiritual war going on against fathers. Because of their role in the family, Satan uses missing fathers to mar children's perspectives on the Heavenly Father. Out of this marred perspective pour broken homes, broken relationships and a broken society.

Let me share a few of the statistics with you. The big picture is that a father matters from the moment of conception and throughout the entire life of the child. According to fatherhood.org, women who have no partner support during their pregnancy are twice as likely to experience miscarriages. The implication of this statistic is that fathers matter before birth and the environment that a pregnant woman spends time in impacts the health of the in-utero baby. Young women who grow up without a father are seven times more likely to experience teen pregnancy. My personal interpretation of this statistic is that a young woman without a father is looking for the image of her Heavenly Father in the men she encounters. This begins with her father, and when he fails her, she turns to other male relationships for identity. This desire to be loved by a man stems from the curse, and it can only be healed by

---

2   Freeman, Mitch. "Father Facts 7 (Download)." FatherSource™. 2015. Accessed May 01, 2019. https://store.fatherhood.org/father-facts-7-download/, 31.

intimate relationship with Jesus. She is hungry for spiritual intimacy, and has not been taught how to encounter the God who created her. She fills that need with physical encounters with the opposite gender.

The greatest indicator that a male child would use alcohol and drugs is fatherlessness. Fatherless boys are more likely to be involved in crime. In fact, children without fathers are 279% more likely to carry guns than their fathered peers. Children in fatherless homes are four times more likely to live in poverty and are twice as likely to experience childhood obesity. Fatherless children were more likely to exhibit destructive or violent behaviors than their peers. They were more likely to need mental health services than other children. In other words, fatherlessness impacts every aspect of a child's life, from mental health to obesity, from birth to adulthood. This is what the research says - scientific research that supports the claims of God's Word - that fathers are a pivotal person in a child's life who is called to reveal God's nature and character to their children. The Scripture looks to fathers as the backbone of society and holds them responsible for its flaws. The Bible also focuses on obedience to fathers and mothers as a means of bringing blessing and healing to individuals and society.

Pay close attention, my child, to your father's wise words and never forget your mother's instructions. For their insight will bring you success, adorning you with grace-filled thoughts and giving you reins to guide your decisions.

Proverbs 1:8-9

Listen to your father who begot you,
And do not despise your mother when she is old.
Buy the truth, and do not sell it,
Also wisdom and instruction and understanding.
The father of the righteous will greatly rejoice,

And he who begets a wise child will delight in him.
Let your father and your mother be glad,
And let her who bore you rejoice.
My son, give me your heart,
And let your eyes observe my ways.

Proverbs 23:22-26

God intended that fathers and mothers would impart wisdom to their children with their presence, their words, and their lifestyle, that would enable children to be successful in a life of obedience to God and service to others. When fathers fail to impart godly lifestyles to their children, these kids grow up to pass on their own dysfunctional ways of living to another generation, and the cycle of brokenness continues.

Not surprisingly, fatherlessness plays a huge role in child abuse. Studies indicate that the presence of an involved father is a deterrent to all forms of abuse. Children who are raised by loving fathers find themselves in less dangerous or exposed situations. These same children know how to use their voices and advocate for themselves, because their fathers have taught them their inner value. However, when the father is missing the likelihood that a child will experience some type of abuse increases greatly.

STORIES OF BROKEN FAMILIES

National statistics show that in over 60 percent of cases, neglect was the reason why a child was placed in foster care and in 36 percent of cases, neglect arose because of addiction[3]. Although the perpetrators of abuse and neglect have broken the

---

3   United States. Department of Health and Human Services. The AF-CARS Report. Washington, D.C.: U.S. Dept. of Health and Human Services, Administration for Children and Families, Administration on Children, Youth and Families, Childrens Bureau.

law and have endangered their children, many of them need our help and support as a community. With assistance, they may have the potential to learn the skills they need to manage their mental health issues, addiction being the greatest. It has been my experience that the many perpetrators are motivated by addiction, and the cycles of brokenness that they have experienced in their own childhoods hold them captive.

It has been a great privilege of my life to mentor the dear lady who gave birth to one of my sons. I remember the first day I met Norma. Our first meeting was at a court date where we both needed to be present in order to change this child's plan from reunification with biological family to adoption. Up until this point, I had dehumanized this person in my mind. She had hurt my child and that was all that mattered to me. My husband, who had met her before, told me she was kind and truly cared about what was best for our child, but I refused to believe him. I did not want to care about the needs or inner pain or potential of this woman. I claimed it was because I could not stand those who hurt my kids, but now I know it was because my heart was full of judgement. I had forgotten my own brokenness and the mercy and grace of God that I had experienced in my life. On the day I met Norma, I remember walking down the hallway toward the courtroom and seeing her for the first time. She seemed nervous and unsure of herself. I felt the pull of the Holy Spirit to walk up to her and introduce myself.

"Hello, my name is Harmony. I am _____ foster mom."

"I'm Norma. It's nice to meet you. Thanks for all you're doing for my son."In that moment, I heard the voice of God. "You know," He said, "She needs a mom, too." I could feel my heart changing in that moment. I felt God opening my eyes to Norma's beautiful soul. I could feel her desperate need for belonging and for love. I could see that, with some help, she might be able to completely change the trajectory of her life. And, I found, that I cared. Suddenly, I wanted to be part of that transformation. I looked within myself and I saw the seeds she needed. I was in the habit of doing this in other arenas of my life. For example, as a wife, I recognize that God often puts within me the words of encouragement, the affection, or the wisdom that my husband needs. I recognize as a teacher that I have huge potential to help students develop their gifts and talents. I can make school a powerful and meaningful experience for students because of the personality, anointing and natural gifting that God put in me. The same is true for my children. Until that moment with Norma, I had never considered that God might use me to reach the biological families of my children. All of a sudden, I saw that I could change more than my son's life. I only had to choose.

I had no idea how much I had to learn from Norma. I did not know in that moment that Norma would become a member of our family and that I would love her like a sister. I did not know that I needed her in my life as much as she needed me. I knew that I wanted to help her and that I could be the tipping point for change in her life, and I chose to take the risk and get involved. We began to have visits outside of the DHS building, where most visits take place between foster kids and their biological families. We would meet at the park or at McDonald's and I would get to watch her interact with our son and with my other children. She treated me with the utmost respect. She referred to me as her son's mom. She supported my discipline and affection toward our shared son. My respect for her grew, as she shared what she had overcome in her life that had brought her to the present moment. As my respect grew, my perspective on biological families began to shift. My compassion was deepened and my understanding of the root causes of abuse and neglect expanded.

Over our two-and-a-half-year friendship, Norma has shared parts of her story with me, and she has given me permission to share them with you. I share them for two reasons: I want your own compassion and understanding to be expanded, and I want you to have a glimpse into what these fathers and mothers have endured themselves that brings them to a place where they cannot care for their own children. It in no way excuses their choices. There are always consequences, and Norma has experienced many sad losses because of her addiction. There are no excuses, but there are reasons, and those reasons need to be acknowledged.

Norma grew up with a single mom who was also an addict. She saw men come and go from her home, but did not know her biological father. Her mother refused to share her father's identity with her, so Norma has never had any contact with him. This was the first and most painful loss of Norma's story. She has always longed to know who her dad is and to experience a type of healing and relationship that can come through reconnection with a father. Norma's mother was like many women, desperate for identity, hungering for intimacy and belonging. She chose to seek fulfillment in other addicts and never sustained healthy relationships. Norma learned how to survive this life from her mother. She learned how to use substances to dull the inner pain. She learned that her only value was as an object for men to lust after. She was looking for a father, but did not know that only the Heavenly Father could heal and restore her identity as an image-bearer of God.

Norma became pregnant at a very young age. At 17 years old, she found herself the mother of a beautiful baby girl. Tragically, her little girl died as an infant, and Norma was plunged into a very dark season in her life. She continued to use until she became pregnant again. Norma has always been a loving and sacrificial person. She demonstrated this inner compass by choosing not to use drugs while she was pregnant. She cared deeply for her babies and did not want her addiction to pass from her to her baby. Again, Norma was looking for identity. She found a sense of worth when she was pregnant, but once the child was born, she would return to using. Her second and third sons were both placed in foster care. The oldest was adopted and the other exhibited high anxiety, sexualized behaviors and aggression. He was moved from home to home, but none could handle his needs. At this point, Norma was pregnant again. She understood that if she did not choose to change her lifestyle, she would lose her fourth child. She desired change and decided to live in a special home where there would be oversight and accountability. Living in the halfway house helped her transition from being pregnant to being a mom without returning to her addiction.

We met Norma while she was living in the halfway house. She was raising her youngest son, and she began attending church with us. She sat with us during service and fit right in with our motley crew. She received Jesus as her personal Lord and Savior and was baptized during this time. Her third son, who had really struggled with behaviors in other homes, began to grow and improve with us, and we chose not to give up on him. Norma also saw the change and growth and was very supportive of our methods. Her youngest son became a nephew to Scott and myself. We had gained so much more than a foster son, and Norma had gained the freedom, relationships and identity that she had always desired.

Norma now lives in her own apartment with her fourth child. She went back to school and became an esthetician. When she was considering going back to school, she shared with me that she had never seen education as an option for her. The word college was never used in her home. She had not excelled in academic settings. She had left high school early and received her GED. She shared some anxiety about returning to school, and I highly encouraged her to take the risk and go to beauty school. I was her cheerleader along the way. When she did not want to fill out the paperwork for beauty school, I pushed her to complete it. When she was afraid, we would pray together. When she wanted to quit, I reminded her what she would gain if she stuck with it. When she was dealing with anxiety around her tests, I would intercede for her. She passed her state tests and became a licensed esthetician, against all odds. Against what she had been taught as a child, against her own view of her intelligence, against everything she had failed at up until that point, Norma succeeded. She now owns her own business.

I share her story, because I want you to know what I did not know when I first became a foster parent. The parents who have lost their children are in need of love. Many of them are fatherless or have strained relationships with their biological families. They did not grow up like I did, surrounded by loved, wanted and important to my parents. Many of them are also victims of abuse and neglect. They have never been exposed to a different way. As I said before, their experiences do not excuse them from responsibility for their actions. But knowing what they have gone through can inform our opinions about them. Just as God saw us as pure and spotless bride, even while we were yet sinners (Romans 5), these adults need someone who can see them as whole and beautiful. They need to be *seen*, not labeled. They need to be called by their heavenly calling, not by their earthly mistakes.

THE COST

The epidemic of fatherlessness is not without a cost. Although the financial cost of fatherlessness is not the most important negative impact on our society, it is important to recognize that our government is trillions of dollars in debt, and part of that debt is because of the breakdown of the family. Father Facts 7[4] reports that fatherless families are more likely to need financial assistance from the government. In 2006 alone, the Feder-

---

4   Freeman, Mitch. "Father Facts 7 (Download)." FatherSource™. 2015. Accessed May 01, 2019. https://store.fatherhood.org/father-facts-7-download/, 31.

al Government spent $99.8 million on single mother families. If Christ-followers chose to take in the fatherless, the financial situation in this country would improve. If we were to raise a generation of sons who are image-bearers of God, who know their identity, these sons would then produce a generation after them who reflect that fathering heart. The Gospel can have a snowball effect that benefits all parts of society, including the government.

Absent fathers are impacting our educational and health care systems as well. Children who are raised without a father are more likely to develop behavioral issues, which hinder both the fatherless child and the learning of other students[5]. I have inside knowledge of this statistic. As a teacher, I have seen firsthand how children without fathers behave. I have daily interactions with children who are being abused or neglected at home. I watch them as they come to school dirty, in clothes either too big or too small. These children hang their heads and refuse to make eye contact. They shy away from contact with other humans because of physical abuse. I have reached out to put my hand on a student's shoulder and had them flinch away as if they were going to be slapped in the face. And I have been slapped in the face by a student whose emotional disruptions have made learning almost impossible for his classmates. The behaviors of these children are just symptoms of a deeper issue - a lack of identity that comes from the orphan spirit.

These fatherless sons and daughters need and receive mental health support in and out of school. We hire counselors, CDS teachers, and TOSA's (Teacher On Special Assignment) just to give our students the social-emotional building blocks that they should have received at home while they were toddlers. As a foster mom, I have seen the counselors' offices full of hurting children and parents in need of resources. As a

---

5   Freeman, Mitch. "Father Facts 7 (Download)." FatherSource™. 2015. Accessed May 01, 2019. https://store.fatherhood.org/father-facts-7-download/, 32.

teacher, my classroom as doubled as a counseling office, as students have poured out their hurt, fears, and confusion to me. In a small way, I choose to be the voice of identity in these students' lives, but I can never replace the missing father they are craving. I believe God uses me in those moments to give them a glimpse of how much their Heavenly Father loves them. I give them a taste so that they continue to seek Him until they find Him. But I have also had these same students tare the posters off my walls and turn over the chairs in my room. I have stood by while a child has screamed at me with no recourse except to wait it out patiently. I have witnessed loving principals and office managers who cannot do their job well because the office is constantly full of broken, hurting souls who cannot function in the regular classroom. And in that moment, I know I am looking at the cost of a fatherless generation.

A CITY ON A HILL

There is no hopeless situation that God has not called us to walk into and invade with His light. Although the situation I have described is dark and it may appear that the kingdom of darkness is having its heyday at the expense of our kids, the truth is Jesus sealed our victory before the foundations of the earth were laid. I tell you these stark, cold facts not to scare you, but to stir your outrage and compassion. There is no need to embellish the darkness, no need to paint it in a more dire light—it is as dire as it has ever been in human history, and yet it has always been this dark. I am asking you to pray about what your part is to be in this dire situation. Will you sit back and leave the darkness for someone else to confront, or will you turn on the light and see the darkness flee? The choice is up to you.

CHAPTER 4

Unconventional Parenthood

With joy, we return to the story of us. We left off at the moment when Brenden became our son. What a beautiful day that was for Scott and me. I remember texting Scott, "You're a father! I'm bringing our son home today!" We had waited so long, it hardly seemed real. But it was. We were not truly prepared for what would ensue over the next few weeks. We were euphoric and full of dreams. Brenden, on the other hand, was not. He did not understand why he had been separated from his caretaker. That first night, he was happy. He received some new things, like a Ninja Turtles blanket and new clothes, and he enjoyed being the center of attention. He was allowed to eat what he wanted for dinner, and he even got to watch a cartoon. In his eyes, we were a fun sleepover. When we did not return him to his caretaker the next day, however, he began to realize things were not going his way. He became afraid and very angry.

When a child of trauma is removed from an unsafe environment, they bring their pain and coping mechanisms with them. Their experiences have given them neuro-pathways in the brain that look different than the brain of a well-loved child and they continue to use those pathways until their brains have been retrained (Child Welfare Information Gateway, 2015), which can take years. Without miraculous intervention, many children never fully recover from their years of trauma. A simple example of this was Brenden's lack of basic social skills that most seven-year-old children possess. Brenden did not say please when he wanted something and he did not show gratitude when we blessed him. He did not know how to show affection in appropriate ways. Brenden did not speak in full sentences when he first came to our home and could not count to 20. He had missed copious days of school, which was one of the red flags that he was a victim of neglect. Brenden's brain had been relying heavily on brain state called *the survival state* (Bailey, 2015). His frontal cortex, the area of this brain where critical thinking is developed, had been completely neglected, because Brenden was not having his basic needs met. Who has time or energy to think critically when he or she has no idea where their next meal is coming from? This was Brenden's reality when he arrived in our home.

Brenden had not been exposed to the language he required to communicate his needs in a respectful and safe manner. The words he did know were not all safe and loving; in fact, many of them were obscene. A child who cannot express themselves with words is left with very few options, and almost all of those options were physical. Because of all of these factors, our parenting needed to be tailor-made to fit Brenden's needs. Parenting a foster child does not look the same as the way moms and dads parent a child that they gave birth to—a child they nursed and potty-trained, a child whose first words of "dada" and "mama" are an expression of their loving and safe environment. In fact, all of those pieces of early childhood development - skin-on-skin contact with safe adults, nutrition, the vestibular stimulation of rocking and bouncing, eye contact, smiles, cuddles, singing, identity words, such as "son" and "baby," were all missing from Brenden's life.

Brenden's mother had died at an early age and his biological father had abandoned him because he did not demonstrate "normal" cognitive development. We could not expect Brenden to relate to us in the manner that one would expect a normally adjusted and well-loved child to relate. If he had exhibited these markers of normal early childhood development, he would probably not have needed intervention from CPS, as these markers are the signs of a safe and loving home. We knew right away that our parenting would entail us giving up our preconceived notions of child-rearing. Growth would need to be defined differently, and both Brenden and we would need a ton of patience and forgiveness along the way.

Brenden was not used to eating food that did not come from a box. He was not accustomed to the taste of unprocessed meat or foods that are grown out of the ground (fruits and veggies). We decided right away that his food choices were not the first priority. We could have tried to fight with him about his food. We could have refused to buy Lunchables and cheese pizza. We decided that for the first three months, we would provide him with meals that were similar to what he had been eating previously, because there were bigger fish to fry. First and foremost, Brenden needed to feel safe and loved so that his brain could operate properly. Scott and I put structures in place in our home that were designed to help Brenden succeed.

ROUTINES

Before he came to live with us, Brenden had been living in a truck with three dogs. He never knew when his next meal would come. The place where he slept was covered in dog feces. His schedule was chaotic at best. He was not taken to school on a regular basis. He was left unattended in the truck while his guardian would work at a gas station. He was drugged with sleeping medications so that his guardian could rest undisturbed. It is important to put ourselves in the shoes of this seven-year-old child and see the world from his perspective. It was a very scary place—a place where dangerous men came and went. It was a place where Brenden saw his guardian assaulted on a regular basis. When Scott and I were first deciding what Brenden needed most in his life, we wanted to create a structure that surrounded Brenden with safety so that he would never experience those feelings of chaos and fear again.

Brenden needed a strict routine in his life that provided him with the safety of knowing what to expect. Brenden needed a clean and warm environment with his own bed and belongings. Brenden needed to go to bed at the same time each night and get up to 12 hours of sleep. During sleep, the human brain generates and learns. Brenden had never experienced natural sleep and we wanted to offer him this. Brenden needed to eat at the same times each day. He needed choices he could rely upon. Brenden needed a routine that included hygiene. When he arrived at our home, he had 11 abscesses in his mouth. He needed to learn to brush his teeth and bathe independently. He quickly showed us that he was capable of self-care when he was given the safe and loving environment he deserved. We created a schedule and pre-taught all of the activities on that plan so that Brenden would know what to expect. He soon submitted to that plan because it gave him a sense of relief and calm.

BOUNDARIES

Before Brenden came to us, he had been exposed to abusive adult relationships. He had lost his mother to cancer and his father had abandoned him. The adults he knew had exposed him to concepts far beyond his comprehension, but his young mind had tried to assimilate those behaviors as normal in order to make sense of his world. For example, it was normal to hit women in Brenden's previous experiences. It was normal to scream and use obscene language to control the environment in Brenden's previous life. He was taught simultaneously that he was the only person that mattered and that he was completely worthless. He brought all of these beliefs and behaviors with him.

Brenden needed to see adults love each other in a sacrificial way. He needed a father and mother whose relationship was sacred and private. Brenden needed parents who put the needs of their spouse above the wants of others. He needed to hear words like, "Your mother is speaking to me, please do not interrupt." Brenden needed to know that his father made his mother the priority in his home. He needed to see his father and mother show affection to each other in appropriate and affirming ways. He needed to know that there can be pure and life-giving affection between adults that results in an environment where children also receive life-giving affirmation and affection.

Brenden needed adults to say "No" to him consistently. Brenden needed expectations clearly communicated to him with both positive and negative consequences outlined for his choices. We created a list of positive choices Brenden could make and a coinciding list of positive consequences that would take place when he made those excellent choices. He could count on us to follow through with those rewards, and that consistency taught him trust. He also fully understood what would happen if he chose to make an unsafe choice, because a list of those was also created, along with the consequence of each choice. These boundaries gave Brenden the freedom of voice and choice. He began to learn how to take control of his life in healthy ways and within the boundaries that were set for him. He had control over the consequences in his life - either positive or negative. He could take personal pride when he earned a positive reward and we taught him to take personal responsibility when he failed. We taught Brenden that failure is inevitable and an opportunity to learn.

COMMUNITY

Before that fateful day when he became our son, Brenden lived on the fringes of society. He was homeless and because of the poor choices of adults in his life, he was chronically truant from school. Because of his speech and socio-emotional delays, he had no friends. Forming connections with other children was almost impossible for a few reasons. First, he was not present in his classroom enough to create strong bonds with other children. Secondly, when he was in school, Brenden tended to express frustration by assaulting other children, which did not encourage them to play with him. Thirdly, and most importantly, Brenden had lost many important relationships which had left him with deep and untreated wounds. Brenden had lost connection with an older brother and sister who were raised by his biological father. His mother and grandmother had died, and his current guardian was riddled with addiction. Even though he was extremely attached to her, she only exacerbated Brenden's conditions and cut him off from people who could provide supports and resources. Brenden's family was not connected to a faith-based community that might have assisted them through hard times. When he came to live with us, he effectively lost the only person left from his former life (his previous guardian). He had lost everyone and everything that given him identity before his eighth birthday.

Scott and I were determined that we would foster important and healthy relationships with members of Brenden's family. Through his social worker, we reached out to his siblings and began phone conversations with them on a regular basis. Brenden's biological father had no interest in a relationship with Brenden, and we did not pursue one with him. We believed, and so did Brenden's therapist, that it was the father's job, not Brenden's, to create and sustain relationship with his son. If he was unwilling, that only demonstrated he had abandoned his post and lost the right to relationship with our son. We encouraged contact between Brenden and his aunts and cousins, as well. As long as these people demonstrated safe behaviors, we wanted Brenden to feel that he had not lost his biological family forever. We wanted him to only gain from his experiences from us. There was a hard balance that must be struck, however, between connection with the biological family and creating something new in Brenden's life that did not constantly pull him back to the brokenness of his past. Many times when foster children have visits with biological family members, there is a recurrence of past behaviors. As well-meaning as those family members may be, they sometimes represent a way of life that was not healthy for the child and may stir up coping strategies that no longer work for the child. We wanted to maintain a healthy connection with Brenden's biological family, while also teaching him a new way of doing life.

Each foster child needs a different level of connection with their birth family, and each birth family will demonstrate differing levels of a safe lifestyle. This can be a painful process for both the child and the foster parents. Speaking from personal experience, it can be extremely painful to feel that the child you love is more attached to the people who abused him than he is to you. It can be hard to "share" the affections of your child, and it is hard to watch them return to unhealthy behaviors each time that he has a visit. The truth is, every child has a need to be loved and embraced by their birth family that can never be fully met by a foster or adoptive mom and dad. The reasons for that go back to God's original intention for His children. He meant for fathers and mothers to show their children his nature and character. When they fail their children, it breaks something deep within the child that can only be healed with repeated exposure to God's loving presence, and the help of loving adults who consistently step up to demonstrate the heart of the Heavenly Father to that hurting child. Even with these ingredients present, the child will have to make a conscious choice to *believe* that the actions of their abusers do not define them.

Building an unconventional family is hard work that takes years. Scott and I have been Brenden's parents for three and a half years, and we are still dealing with behaviors that are directly tied to his past life. He has grown leaps and bounds, but he will always have hurdles in front of him that other children do not face, and our family has to be prepared for those challenges. Every day, we work on our connection with our children, expressing love for them, setting firm boundaries that make them feel safe and impressing upon them their importance to God and to us. Because of Brenden's need for community, and because of the prophetic word that God had released over us, we knew that more children would be coming into our lives that would offer Brenden expanded opportunities for connection. We have been intentional about fostering loving relationships between Brenden and each foster brother or sister, as they have come into our home. We do this because we want our children's lives to feel as fulfilling as possible. His foster siblings did not replace his birth brother and sister, but they have helped to provide joy where there has been loss and belonging where there has been separation. We have done this work, even while we continued to have video chats with his biological siblings and invite them to our home periodically.

We spend a lot of time focusing on our home and the life within it, to the exclusion of distractions that detract. That means we sometimes say "no" to outside activities that would make sense for other people. Nothing is more important to the recovery of our children than their experiences within our walls. That means, we take time to stay home, play outside, read books to our children, build things with our hands and just enjoy each other's company. Once the inner circle of family is established, there are secondary relationships that are also important to a foster child, but those relationships must come after their feelings of chaos and fear have somewhat abated. They learn first how to interact with the members of the healthy family, and as a bi-product, our children can then build safe and kind relationships outside of our home. The arena that springs to mind immediately is the environment of school. Children spend eight hours a day in the care of school staff. That staff can become like a second family to the child. It is extremely valuable for foster families to cultivate relationships with the child's classroom teacher, communicating with them the specific needs of the child. Because I worked at the school where Brenden attended, I had established connections with his teachers already. I was excited to encourage Brenden's academic growth. I knew that as Brenden experienced safety and support at home, his academic capacities would increase. I made it my job to communicate his needs to his educators and to gather feedback from them about his interactions at school. I made myself fully available to them and we worked together for Brenden's success. We have continued this relationship throughout the last three years, and it has had a major impact on Brenden's psyche. Where he felt disconnected and alone when he first came to us, now he feels important in his sphere of influence. He went from being extremely needy to being a young man who was ready to give to others. This shift was fostered by Scott and myself and by the staff at Brenden's elementary school, and without their help, Brenden would never have experienced his current level of success.

The church is the third sphere of community that has come to have significant value for Brenden. The members of our church have made our children their business. They have sown time, energy and resources into us and have been present for us when we were most desperate for help. When Brenden first came to live with us, he had never attended church and did not know the expected behaviors of that environment. Even though Brenden was overwhelmed by a new situation and expressed his feelings in unconventional and unhelpful ways, the teachers in our children's department embraced and supported him through his process. They asked important questions about his emotional needs, and we provided them with information so that both the teachers and Brenden could grow and learn from each other. Although many of these teachers had never experienced a child with such high needs, they saw it as an opportunity to learn how to better minister to their community by opening their doors to every type of child. Because they chose to see past the outward expression of his inner turmoil, Brenden grew to love the teachers in our children's department and to view them as mentors. He has held onto and cultivated his church relationships, taking personal responsibility and contributing to the success of other children.

Because we live 2,600 miles away from our parents, there have been times when we have felt alone on this journey. Our inner circle, which would normally include loving grandparents, uncles and aunts who would support us and help us raise our family, was living in Wisconsin, while God had called us to Oregon. In a small way, Scott and I needed God to set us in a family, as he had set Brenden in ours. He was faithful to do so. There have been three significant families who have courageously served us and welcomed us into their inner circle. These families watch our children free of charge so that Scott and I can get some alone time. These families pour out blessings on our kids when a birthday or "Gotcha Day" arises. When one of my children exhibits unhealthy behaviors, they do not throw up their hands and give up on my child. Instead, these three families have loved my children as we love them.

I share this information about community with you on purpose. None of us do this work alone. We are not called to do it alone. If we look at the structures put in place in the Scripture, we see that God never intended for any of us to be a lone ranger. Instead, we are parts of one body, joined together to add what we have been given to the overall health of everyone else. We are one building, with Jesus Christ as our foundation, and each concrete block, each window, each eave, has an important job that no one else could do. Brenden was not the only one who needed a strong and stable community that offered him love, accountability and support. Each of us has this same need to be fitly joined to others in unity. It is such a relief to know that God has not called me to do everything. Even in the lives of my children, there are so many God-ingredients that come from other people's hands.

Coming to Him as to a living stone, rejected indeed by men, but chosen by God and precious, you also, as living stones, are being built up a spiritual house, a holy priesthood, to offer up spiritual sacrifices acceptable to God through Jesus Christ. Therefore it is also contained in the Scripture, "Behold, I lay in Zion a chief cornerstone, elect, precious, and he who believes on Him will by no means be put to shame."

1 Peter 2:4-6 (NKJV)

IDENTITY

Perhaps the most important structure that we consistently give to Brenden and to all our children is the God-prescribed format for *identity*. Our children come to us asking themselves and others, "Who am I?" Many will have voices in their heads; tapes on repeat that inform them they have no worth. They will look back at the way they have been treated and feel that their circumstances confirm those sickening tracks playing in their minds. Then they turn to us as if to ask, "Is what I feel really true? Did I deserve to get beat up? Did I ask to be molested? Did I ruin my parents' lives?" The truth is, other adults have told our children these lies. Other adults, the adults who were supposed to protect them, who were supposed to show our children the very face of God, have instead showed them the face of evil. Now they look to us and ask, "Were those adults right about me?" They may not ask us these questions with their words. They may never say these things aloud. It may take years for them to open up about the abuse they have experienced. Whether they say a word or not, however, each child will *show us* his or her questions with their actions. Each time they run away, or break something valuable on purpose, or strike another child without cause, they are asking, "Am I worthless? Will you reject me as well?"

Then He took a little child and set him in the midst of them. And when He had taken him in His arms, He said to them, "Whoever receives one of these little children in My name receives Me; and whoever receives Me, receives not Me but Him who sent Me."

Mark 9:36-37 (NKJV)

To receive one of these children is to receive God Himself. Let that sink in past fear, past unbelief, past religion. We must not be like the disciples who were literally hindering children from experiencing the face-to-face presence of the Messiah. Instead we are called to offer them that cleansing stream we have all experienced. We step into his presence, like a running stream of the purest water, and we come out clean and refreshed. Water does not merely scour the outside. It is the drink of life because our very cells are made of water. We step into the water of His Word, and Jesus washes the outside while giving resurrection life to the inside of us as well. When Brenden came to us, he was covered in the filth that adults had thrown on him. He needed the fresh water of Jesus' love. He needed to drink deeply of God's image, so that his very cells would be awakened to his identity. When Brenden would test our limits with dangerous or disrespectful behavior, he was giving us an opportunity to either behave like those first adults, or to let the stream flow out of us and into him.

Like the men we discussed from the book of Genesis,

Brenden had experienced the rejection of his earthly father. When he first came to stay with us, he could not put into words what had happened to him, but he knew his biological dad did not want him. He said, "My dad doesn't want me." Over time, he gained the language he needed to communicate his experience. Brenden told us about the day his biological father came to pick up his brother and sister. Brenden's mother had just passed away, and they were staying with an aunt. As they stood there in the living room discussing what was going to happen next, Brenden's birth dad said, "I'll take the older two, but I won't take Brenden. I don't want to raise a child with his problems. He's probably not mine, anyway." Brenden was present when his earthly father said those wretched words. They impressed upon Brenden that he was something to throw away. Because of this experience, Brenden needed a strong and loving father, affectionate and present, to undo the cruelty he had already lived through.

God's design puts fathers at the forefront of His format for identity, because God Himself is a Father. Men must recognize this truth and embody the challenge. Instead of questioning God's design, they must bring their thoughts into agreement with God's Word. Scott has had a huge role in developing Brenden's identity as an image bearer of God. Each night, Scott goes into Brenden's room and lays his hands on Brenden's head. Scott has Brenden repeat statements that impress upon his mind what God says about him. "I am a son of God. I belong in God's family and in the Klingenmeyer family. I am smart, strong and compassionate. I care about others the way that God cares about me. I am special to Dad and Mom." These confessions help overwrite the recordings playing in our child's mind. Brenden hears a father's audible voice speak worth and godliness over him. In the beginning, Brenden did not agree with the statements that Scott declared over his life, and his behavior continued to reflect his beliefs. Scott and I both believed that actions would bring Scott's words to life in our son. In the same way that God is the great Promise Keeper, the One who speaks and performs His Words, so that none of them return void, Scott has striven to show Brenden's great value through actions. Scott has always showered Brenden with time, energy and resources. He has shown up to Brenden's school events and taekwondo tournaments. He has always shown him affection through hugs. Scott takes time to play with Brenden and our other children, making time for the activities that they love. Because of Scott's conscious effort, Brenden has learned to believe what Scott says about him. In Brenden's life, Scott has become a reflection of the greatest Promise Keeper of all.

Scott is also human and flawed. He fails and has opportunities to demonstrate to his family that he needs God's presence and grace to live. He and I both are in the habit of owning our mistakes and repenting to God and each other *in front* of our kids. We set the example. Failure is part of being human. We choose not to hide and blame others, like the first humans did. Instead, we run into the love of Christ, allow him to wash us with His blood. We start fresh, humble and grateful. This example is just as important as the example of doing what is right. Children who have been abused often hurt themselves and others. Perfection is not possible for them. They need to know that *when* they sin, God still loves them. They need to believe that *when* they wake up in a pig pen, as the prodigal son did, and *when* they realize it is so good to return to their Father's home, that they will run without fear to a God who is running out to meet them with open arms.

Another identity building block that we rely heavily on is the Bible. Although we do not force our foster children to read the Scriptures, we have made it a habit to read the Bible in front of them and to them. Each morning, we read the Scriptures together and pray as a family. Scott and I actively prophesy the Word of God over our children. We take scripture verses and insert our children's names into the verse. For example, I love to pray Ephesians 1:3-4 over my kids:

Every spiritual blessing in the heavenly realm has already been lavished upon Brenden as a love gift from our wonderful heavenly Father, the Father of our Lord Jesus—all because he sees us wrapped into Christ. This is why we celebrate him with all our hearts! And he chose Brenden to be his very own, joining Brenden to himself even before he laid the foundation of the universe! Because of his great love, he ordained Brenden, so that he would be seen as holy in his eyes with an unstained innocence. (TPT)

These verses are a slap in the face of rejection and abandonment. They cry out, "You are loved by a Heavenly Father" to every orphan who hears them. We teach our children to question the lies, instead of questioning God's Word, and to respond with the Scripture when the enemy attacks them. You may be wondering if it works. Does reading the Bible with a child change their thinking? I have a two-fold response for you. My first response is, yes, the Scripture has the power to change the minds of children and adults everywhere. My second response is, consistency is the key to true transformation.

"This Book of the Law shall not depart from your mouth, but you shall meditate in it day and night, that you may observe to do according to all that is written in it. For then you will make your way prosperous, and then you will have good success. Have I not commanded you? Be strong and of good courage; do not be afraid, nor be dismayed, for the Lord your God is with you wherever you go."

Joshua 1:8-9 (NKJV)

God gives Joshua the key to victory, the same key to victory that Jesus used so skillfully in the desert when he was tempted by Satan. God tells Joshua, "Let your mouth be full of My Word. Let your mind be set upon my commands. If you do this, you will be prosperous and successful." There is nothing impossible for the person whose mind is fixed on the Word. This is what we teach our children, and like Joshua, like each of us, there are conflicting voices that try to take our thoughts, words and deeds out of alignment with God's truth. We teach our children to hold these thoughts at sword point. We train our children to cast down vain imaginations that degrade their position in Christ. We practice this by speaking the Scripture over our children and having them speak the Scripture over themselves and others. With time, we have seen a shift in our children because of these practices.

THE HEARTBREAK

After reading the above sections, you may be thinking to yourself, "These structures make sense for any family or child. How does foster parenting differ from parenting birth children if the ingredients for success look so similar?" This is a very good point. Good parenting is good parenting. Routines, boundaries, community and identity are really keys to the success of any household. We encourage families everywhere, whether foster, adoptive or birth, to apply these principles and see change in the patterns of behavior in their children. For example, if you find that your child struggles in the morning with following directions and every morning is a painful process to get your child out the door to school, we would suggest to you that your child needs more sleep. Children need a bedtime routine that includes physical calm, connection and affection, and hygiene. Children sleep better when they are clean and feel safe and loved. This is an example of a structure that can be applied to every home and be a benefit to every child.

There are two main differences between foster/adoptive children and birth children: 1) the number of wounds these children bring with them and how they express those wounds; and 2) what your response should be. You may have all the structures in the world in place, and that child might still break your grandmother's china in their first week with you. You might provide them with healthy and delicious food that most children would enjoy, and they may throw it in your face (I am not speaking figuratively here!). You may show your foster child healthy affection and they may still try to hit you or another child. They may act out sexually toward you or another child because of what they have endured. The question is, *when* these behaviors occur, what will the adult response be? There is no question that these children *will* act out. They have been taught coping mechanisms that have helped them survive in the past. Now they are in your home, where what was normal for them is frowned upon, and it will take time to teach them new ways of relating to their world. These behaviors will disgust you and keep you up at night, and the question is, what will you do *when* they happen?

These children will break your heart. They will reject your love. They will hurt others in the same ways that they have been hurt. Can you love them the way that the Father has loved you? Because this love is why God has brought them to you. Every day, we live the story of the prodigal son. When our 12-year-old daughter ran away from home, and we drove the streets looking for her, we were experiencing the excruciating pain that God knows every day because of a world full of wayward children. Because of God's faithfulness, we found her before she experienced any more abuse or pain. When I got the phone call that she was found, I sat in my truck and cried. I knew that I was feeling the heart of God for the salvation of even one lost soul. He truly does leave the 99 to seek the one sheep that has wandered from the safety of His love.

What about when that child does not want your love? Can you continue to pour it out? You might be reading these words and thinking to yourself, I could not handle that rejection. I could not love a person who consistently rejected me. That must be a job for someone more mature than I am. I want to share an uncomfortable truth with you: the call to love the least and lost of this world is the call of every believer, not just those who are foster parents. It is not just the call of those who feel up to the challenge. Love is the command, because God is love.

Those who are loved by God, let his love continually pour from you to one another, because God is love. Everyone who loves is fathered by God and experiences an intimate knowledge of him. The one who doesn't love has yet to know God, for God is love. The light of God's love shined within us when he sent his matchless Son into the world so that we might live through him. This is love: He loved us long before we loved him. It was his love, not ours. He proved it by sending his Son to be the pleasing sacrificial offering to take away our sins.

1 John 4:7-10 (TPT)

You and I have been fathered by God and we have experienced His matchless love. How deeply I believe this to be true, and yet there are still days when my love for others falls short of His glorious, endless love. In those moments I am reflecting the lie of fatherlessness that impacted my life at a very young age. Both Scott and I revert to those old fatherless habits at times, and have to humble ourselves before God, each other and our children. Even in our weakness, the call remains the same: to love others, just as He has loved us. That day when I embraced my daughter in my arms again, she was still sullen, angry that she had been dragged back to our home, angry that she had not escaped from the very people who were keeping her alive. Even though I was astonished that she did not recognize how blessed she was, God gave me love for her that overcame her arrogant heart. I held her even while she was furious with me, and I could feel her heart start to turn. She knew that even though she had broken our trust, even though she had stolen from us and hurt our family, she would never be cast out.

REDEFINING MINISTRY

This love we show our children is a supernatural kind of love. For us, supernatural family means an expression of heavenly love in the face of impossible circumstances and painful rejection. There are days when we echo the words of Jesus in our hearts, "Do you also want to leave (John 6:67)?" Jesus' controversial statements about eating His flesh and drinking His blood drove the fair-weather multitudes away from him. Jesus asked his disciples if they would also abandon Him. When a child is screaming at us that we are not real parents and that he or she hates us and does not want to live with us, our hearts ache within us. With supernatural strength, we take a break and breathe through those circumstances. We go and look at ourselves in the mirror and remember what God has asked us to do. We remind ourselves that the calling is not so small that we can throw it away when we are attacked. With this mindset, we can approach our children and say, "You may hate me today, but I will love you forever. And, one day, you will change your mind about me." I have seen this statement totally melt a hard heart. When the child knows there is nothing they can do to stop you from loving them, the fear of rejection begins to fade and belonging begins to grow.

Scott and I are missionaries to our community. What we do with children is a public service that improves our schools and communities. We are changing the trajectory of families by introducing them to a different way of doing life. We are teaching children who would have otherwise turned to addiction to manage their stress how to function and cope in healthy ways that will not destroy their lives. We are breaking the cycles of abuse that would have continued without our intervention. We are training our children how to parent with love. We are an evangelical force for the Gospel of Jesus Christ. Although we do not force our faith on our children, we invite them into an intimate encounter with their Creator that will change them forever. We invite them to learn of His ways, and once they have had a taste, they never want to go back. If Scott gets busy and forgets to pray over one of the children, they rush out and inform him that they want his prayers. If I am busy in the morning and miss our usual reading and prayer, one of our kids will ask, "Mom, when are we going to read the Bible?" They hunger for it and find fulfillment and safety in it. They come away from these moments with a confidence boosting knowledge that they are children of God. That is our ministry.

This is a word of encouragement to all parents, whether birth, foster or adoptive. What you do at home with your children is the single most impactful ministry you will ever have. There is nothing more powerful than raising up a generation of image-bearers who know they are sons and daughters of the King. If you are a stay-at-home parent, and there are days when you wonder if what you do has value, remember this: Billy Graham's mother may have never preached from the stage. She may have never led another person in the sinner's prayer. She may have been only a homemaker who raised Billy Graham. And because she raised him, she changed the world.

You have the ability to raise world changers. You decide today what atmosphere you are creating in your home. Our children will learn to reflect that atmosphere and carry it with them throughout their days and years. If you choose to foster and adopt, you are choosing to rewrite the stories of more than one family. You are offering this next generation a restart button. Because of your intervention, these children may be the last to experience neglect or abuse in their family lines. You are walking in the footsteps of the Good Shepherd, who laid down his life for the sheep.

"I am the good shepherd. The good shepherd gives His life for the sheep. But a hireling, he who is not the shepherd, one who does not own the sheep, sees the wolf coming and leaves the sheep and flees; and the wolf catches the sheep and scatters them. The hireling flees because he is a hireling and does not care about the sheep. I am the good shepherd; and I know My sheep, and am known by My own. As the Father knows Me, even so I know the Father; and I lay down My life for the sheep. And other sheep I have which are not of this fold; them also I must bring, and they will hear My voice; and there will be one flock and one shepherd. Therefore My Father loves Me, because I lay down My life that I may take it again. No one takes it from Me, but I lay it down of Myself. I have power to lay it down, and I have power to take it again. This command I have received from My Father."

John 10:11-18 (NKJV)

Scott and I choose to reflect the nature of Jesus by acting like the Shepherd and not like a hireling. We choose not to run for cover when things get messy. We choose to forgive our children when they open the door for the enemy to come into our home and we stand guard over their hearts and minds and send the demons running when they come against our kids. We lay down our lives, imperfect as they are, for the children in our care, believing that God takes our sacrifice and makes it holy. He can use us, even us, to shepherd his dear ones. The Father can and will take your life and use it to shepherd His flock, if only you are willing.

THE KLINGENMEYERS

We are in the middle of our story as parents. There may come a day when I look back at what I wrote in these pages and think to myself, "There's so much more to say!" or, "I think I should have left that out!" Scott and I do not have all the answers and we fail on a daily basis. We use trial and error, as all parents do, and have made more errors than we would like to admit. We have also experienced huge triumphs with our children. Brenden, who could not tie his shoes or count to 20 when first he came to us, now reads at a fourth-grade level (he is about to end his fifth-grade year). Each of our children has grown and succeeded in important ways in our home. We believe that they will continue to do so because of God's mercy and His presence that surrounds our children and us. We have learned to rely on Him, to press into Him and to make unity with Him our greatest aim. The benefits of our intimate relationship with God show in the lives of our children as they develop that same intimate connection for themselves.

It is important to add that we do not require our children to agree with the tenants of the Christian faith. No one has ever truly met God through force. We have no intention of demanding belief from our children. Instead of commanding them to believe God's Word or to accept Jesus as their Savior, we have opened up the windows of our own personal relationship with Jesus, so that our children can see inside. They look in and they see love and acceptance. They look in and they see the strength to overcome. They look in and see freedom from fear and addiction. They look into the intimacy we have with Jesus and they decide for themselves that His love is all that can satisfy the inner cry of their hearts. Each of my children has come to me on their own and asked how they can know this Jesus we serve. And we willingly introduced them to their Heavenly Father. We have the privilege of walking down the road of discipleship with them, teaching them how to know

Him better, how to experience Him in the sorrow and storm, how to lean on Him for their every need—how to trust them. As we do this, we ourselves grow to know Him better.

We are on a journey together with our children and with our community, and that journey will not cease until we step into Heaven. We pray that our story will be the very prophetic inspiration in your lives that we ourselves experienced.

CHAPTER 5

A Power Team

The first human relationship that God created was marriage. Marriage was instituted before sin, before shame, before fear entered the picture. Marriage was God's solution to Adam's aloneness. Eve was God's response to the statement, "It is not good for man to be alone." This statement is an important one in the Scripture. In the first chapter of Genesis, God calls each of His creations "good." When He arrives at His image-bearer, the Father calls man "very good." After God has spent so much time pronouncing His creation "good", we have the first mention of something that is not good. That thing that God identified as not good was Adam living without a partner comparable to him. This makes sense if we set the definition of "good" to mean, each created being fulfilling its designed purpose. Man was designed to reflect God. If God Himself lives within a family unit, then in order to fully reflect God, man must also live within a family unit. If the Trinity lives and works within unity to bring about the plans of the Father, then God's image bearer must do the same. When God identifies Adam's aloneness as "not good," He was telling us that outside of community, we cannot fully reflect His nature and character.

I want to share a truth with you that may make you uncomfortable. After your personal relationship with God, your marriage is your first priority. It comes before your children. It comes before your work or your church. Your marriage is your first stewardship and it is meant to be an act of worship to the Father. Many of you might be thinking, I worship God in many ways. I tithe, I sing songs to God, I give to the poor. These are all valuable ways of worshiping, but they are not your first stewardship. There was no need for sacrifice before the fall, but God created marriage apart from sin to reflect His nature and character. There is no record of Adam and Eve singing songs of worship to the Father (although one might imagine that they joined with the heavenly chorus of angels and with the stars that worship the Lord continually). But there *is* a record of God's command to leave and cleave to a wife. The first act of worship, therefore, was intimacy—a face-to-face intimacy with God and with that perfect partner God created for Adam. It was the same unity that exists within the Godhead. Our greatest act of worship is to fulfill our God-prescribed design by reflecting God's nature and character to the world around us. We do this job of reflecting by walking in unity with our spouse.

Scott and I have had to learn this lesson the hard way. We jealously guard our marriage now, but we have not always done so. We have learned the hard way that our marriage must be the center point of our home, and what we have learned about marriage has made our job as foster and adoptive parents easier. It has added to the sense of security and love that our children feel in our home. We have learned that the peace of our home is a reflection of the peace in our marriage. We learned this by dealing with the consequences of our own disobedience. We share with you the lessons we have learned in the hopes that we will make the rough places smoother and the crooked places straighter for you.

THE POWER OF A HARMONIOUS MARRIAGE

Scott and I are as different as two people can be. Scott is a thinker. He enjoys thinking long about a subject, and it can take days for him to formulate a response to a situation. In my brain, thinking and speaking form one continuous loop. I have no problem thinking about a subject, framing what I want to say in a concise way and then speaking what I am thinking—all within milliseconds of each other. Scott's preferred learning style is by doing. In order to learn a new skill, he needs to see it done, then do it for himself. I, on the other hand, learn by listening. I am auditory in nature and interact with my world through sound. I am sure you can see where conflict might arise. Scott thinks instead of speaking. I learn by hearing. This is only a small taste of our differences. Scott is frugal and down-to-earth in his approach to spending. He will wear the same clothes for years without ever thinking that he might benefit from a new outfit. My love language is gifts, and I enjoy blessing others and giving to charitable causes. I get a thrill from a new pair of white sneakers, while Scott gets a thrill from making his old, stained boots last another month. In the first few years of our marriage, we had many misunderstandings tied to these differences.

When I met Scott, I knew right away that I could benefit from his personality. Scott did not believe in credit cards. At 30 years old, Scott owned a home and a truck, and those were his only monthly debt payments. He bought my engagement ring outright with cash. At 26 years old, I had already gone through a huge financial crisis. I had paid off six maxed-out credit cards, and I knew that the man God would bring into my life would have financial wisdom I lacked. Scott also had areas of his life where he needed development. Scott had never experienced emotional and spiritual intimacy with a woman, because he had not seen that demonstrated by the men in his family. When he met me, he began to feel the stirring of a desire to be transparent and vulnerable with a woman in a way he had not known before. Scott and I were both looking for partner who would complement our strengths instead of mirroring them.

Like many people, however, I had weaknesses and areas for development in my character that I did not see. I had a blind spot about my own frailty, and God sent Scott into my life to help strengthen me in my hidden weaknesses, along with the obvious ones. Over time, Scott's frugality began to appear like stinginess to me. I resented his focus on saving money because it exposed my habit of spending thoughtlessly on things I really did not need. I did not value his intentional preparation for our future, because I was looking for fulfillment in the now. The same was true of Scott in the area of priorities and intimacy. Scott and I were married in September, and as any new bride would, I wanted my husband to stay home and invest in his marriage. I needed quality time with him to develop a deeper intimate connection with him. Scott resented my desire for emotional intimacy. He would mock and belittle any attempt at transparency because it made him uncomfortable to be exposed to another human that might reject him. Scott had no desire to invest at home because it was hunting season. He had spent every fall hunting with his family since he was three years old, and he could not fathom why he would change that habit now.

Scott and I both carried wounds from past relationships that hindered our intimacy, love and respect for one another. It took me many years to realize that I had been desperate for affection and attention, because I had experienced human abandonment more than once in my life. Instead of seeking intimacy with Jesus that would lead to meaningful intimacy with my husband, I demanded that Scott show me a depth of love only Christ could. Scott was overwhelmed by my needs, and instead of making an effort, withdrew completely to what was safe and standard for him. Neither of us were experiencing a fulfilling marriage because each of us had expectations of the other that could only be met by Jesus.

Scott and I have learned over the course of our marriage that we were never meant to be the same. We are meant to be a symphony. The beauty of an orchestra comes from its many voices sounding in harmony with one another to touch and stir our deepest emotions. I love the metaphor of instruments to explain the beauty that God intended for marriage. If all the violas play middle C, it may be a beautiful sound (especially if they are in perfect unison), but their sound will have no depth. If the contrabasses begin to play a low A, however, suddenly a deep melancholy feeling will rise up in the heart of the listener. Why does the introduction of another low pitch shift the emotions of the hearer? It is because pitches working together mimic the intimacy that is found within our familial God, the Trinity, in a way that unison never can. It is the same deep emotion we feel when we hear humpback whales sing together. All of creation is imitating the Creator's heartbeat. We were created to imitate His harmony as well.

The longer we spent together, the more obvious our differences became. At first, we were shocked and often disgusted by the differences we discovered in each other. I had no concept that each difference in Scott was meant to harmonize with my unique personality traits. At first, I tried very hard to change Scott from a contrabass to a viola. Why could he not understand the benefit of seeing the world like I did? But can you imagine two of me in the same house? What a noise that would be - like a concert of ill-tuned stringed instruments, all playing the same melody, and all vying to be heard above the din. Instead of a cacophony of jostling sounds, my clear alto voice can be heard, no matter how many instruments may be playing, because there is only one me. Likewise, Scott releases a unique sound into the atmosphere, and his sound is his own and no one else's. Together, our personalities are meant to lift up the sound of the other, instead of overpowering our partner. God has opened my eyes to my need for Scott to be exactly who he is in order for my personality to be what God intended it to be.

I am still tempted on occasion to try to force Scott into

a box I have created for him. I have found, however, that as I leave Scott alone to be who he is, God Himself does the fine tuning. Scott has changed, that is for certain, and not because I forced him to, or he finally gave in to all my pushing. As Scott has spent time with the Master Craftsman, Scott's personality has become gentler, kinder, and more intimate. Being a father to wounded children has taken Scott to the Potter's wheel for some reworking. Scott's desire to be a loving father has been a driving force for maturity in his life and has encouraged Scott to spend more time in God's presence learning who his Heavenly Father is. Scott's identity as an image-bearer of God was always within him. He just needed time with the Father to discover who he really was. The same is true in the case of my rough edges. As I have chosen to seek intimacy with Jesus as my first priority, He has sharpened and smoothed me. I have learned that lecturing and badgering only produces bitterness. I have learned that love, service, and a voice that speaks prophetically are the tools to changing an atmosphere. God has changed me, not because Scott wanted me to change, but because His presence transforms us to reflect God's nature and character.

When the melodies start to clash in my home again, I take a deep breath and ask myself this question: Am I trying to make my spouse or children sound like me? Am I giving them the freedom to experience the fruit of their choices, both good and bad, without trying to control every outcome for them? Both my husband and my children need the freedom to express themselves. That is when the most beautiful music is made. That is when our lives become a worship symphony to God.

As a prisoner of the Lord, I plead with you to walk holy, in a way that is suitable to your high rank, given to you in your divine calling. With tender humility and quiet patience, always demonstrate gentleness and generous love

toward one another, especially toward those who may try
your patience. Be faithful to guard the sweet harmony of
the Holy Spirit among you in the bonds of peace, being one
body and one spirit, as you were all called into the same
glorious hope of divine destiny.

Ephesians 4:1-4 (TPT)

THE POWER OF FAILURE

As a music teacher, I am constantly telling my students, "Leaders take risks, and risk takers make mistakes. Our goal can never be perfection, because none of us is perfect. Our goal is to confidently fail so that we can grow." I carry this belief into every part of my life. Failure is the ailment of the bold, and I want to be bold. I want to face every challenge with my eyes open and with courage. Because of past failure, I knew that marriage would be difficult for me. I knew that my heart had already been broken and that the wounds were healing, but the scars remained. I also knew that God was calling me to this marriage. God's voice had birthed our relationship and I have been in the habit of following God's voice. I also knew that marrying Scott would teach me lessons I could not learn any other way, and I desired to grow in God. I knew I would fail, but I jumped in anyway, because I believe failure leads to success.

Scott was not my first husband. I was married once before when I was young, and that relationship had been full of physical abuse and unfaithfulness. My previous husband and I were part of a religious organization that encouraged him to beat me. He did not keep his marriage vows but engaged in illicit relationships with other women. Those wounds were deep, and their presence made it difficult for me to trust men. They also left me in a place where I was longing for the affection and attention of a man who might show me Christ's love. When I met Scott, I encountered that love, but I also encountered another broken human being in need of healing. Scott had been engaged twice before, and had sustained some hurts from those relationships. Even though we knew we would fail, we embarked on a journey together - a covenant journey that will last a lifetime, a journey that is written one day at a time, one failure at a time, one victory at a time.

The word failure is an unfriendly word. It makes us uncomfortable because we have been brainwashed by society to believe failure and the product of failure—brokenness, repentance, and humility—are unnecessary vices of religion. The truth is, the Bible is full of powerful stories of men and women who failed, and then rose victorious to change the world. Think of Peter - the man who denied Jesus three times on the night the Messiah was betrayed. This same man jumped out of a boat and swam to Jesus when He was raised from the dead. Yes, he had failed. But Peter knew that his only hope was to humble himself before the Lord. This same man preached to thousands of people on the day of Pentecost and 3,000 were added to God's Kingdom that day. Think of Rahab, the harlot of Jericho. She was a woman of the night. She was also the only one with the discernment to offer shelter to the Israelite men who scoped out the city. Rahab knew her only hope was to plead for her life and the lives of her family from the men she had protected. She boldly put out her scarlet thread and changed her life and the lives of everyone in her family. She married a man of Israel and is named in the lineage of Jesus. Rahab was the mother of Boaz, the kinsman redeemer of the book of Ruth, and the great-grandfather of King David. Rahab is mentioned in "faith chapter," Hebrews 11, along with a veritable list of failures. Abraham, who sent his son into the desert to die, Sarah, who laughed at the promises of God, and Moses, who was a murderer, all make the list of faith giants. What is God saying? He means to use our failures for our good and His glory. No moment of our lives will be wasted. And He will use our cave experiences to make us into kings.

So we are convinced that every detail of our lives is continually woven together to fit into God's perfect plan of bringing good into our lives, for we are his lovers who have been called to fulfill his designed purpose. For he knew all about us before we were born and he destined us from the beginning to share the likeness of his Son. This means the Son is the oldest among a vast family of brothers and sisters who will become just like him.

Romans 8:28-29 (TPT)

Every detail of our lives is being woven together for the Father's purposes. I believe that this weaving includes our failures. I believe it includes moments of brokenness and humility. Let me clarify by saying, I do not believe it is God's will that we sin. Sin and failure are not synonymous in definition. It is possible to fail in many ways that are not sinful. For example, it is possible to try to start a new business and see that business fail. It is possible to invest in a stock and see it fail. It is possible to start a new ministry and see it fail. In my classroom, I see these types of failures every day. A child tries to play a new instrument and they make lots of lovely mistakes that help them grow. My son makes mistakes when he reads material above his academic level and he comes across new words he has never seen before. He may read them incorrectly the first time, but with some assistance, he may read them correctly the next time they pop up. God is in these types of failures. They teach us to trust Him, how to hear His voice more clearly and how to try again when we get it wrong. Proverbs 24:16 says, "For a righteous man may fall seven times and rise again, but the wicked shall fall by calamity." This is so true of the courageous person who takes risks.

However, I look back at the lives of Peter and Abraham and Rahab, and I see the evidence of a God who also uses our sinful failures to produce humility and submission to the Spirit in His children. If we are teachable, the Father can use any moment as a learning moment, and He is more than willing to take what the enemy meant for our destruction and use it to make us more dependent on His Spirit. When I was in that first marriage, a horrible mistake of disobedience to God, I had no idea how the Father would use my brokenness to create in me a humble and teachable heart. In spite of our weaknesses, God is able to work ALL things to our benefit and His glory. This is the beautiful testimony of my marriage to Scott. We have failed, and God has used our failure to teach us obedience. He has used our circumstances to discipline us.

What does this look like in a practical sense? It looks like our children parroting petty and selfish arguments. It looks like brothers and sisters at each other's throats instead of playing and having fun with one another. Scott and I used to bicker quite a bit. We have passionate personalities that enjoy being right. There were times when we would fight about small things, bantering back and forth. Sometimes those arguments would get heated and the children would hear us. Usually within 24 hours, we would see our children engaging in the same kinds of conversations. We would look at each other with knowing in our eyes. We have learned to go to our children and ask their forgiveness for arguing in ways that are not loving. The children are very responsive to humility and will often improve their behaviors quite quickly. Children are the mirrors of their environment. Because my children come to me with trauma and mental illness, we often have to deal with the roots of behaviors that did not get planted in our home. However, there are times when I see my own stubbornness and selfishness in the eyes of my children, and I remind myself that I too am not without sin. I pray that the Holy Spirit will always convict me and that I will quickly repent and submit to the Lord, so that my children will learn to do the same. Failure is inevitable, and it is important we know how to humble ourselves and make it right.

David shows us the power of transparent humility in the Psalms. He is brutally honest about his failures and even more about his need for the assistance of the Holy Spirit. The Psalms give us a handbook of how to handle our own brokenness. Children need to know that when they fail, they can run directly into the arms of God. Mothers and fathers are called to demonstrate this kind of humility openly before their children so that the next generation knows how to repent and receive mercy and grace. If we only repent in private, then others will never learn how to come clean before God. James 5:16 commands us, "Confess your trespasses to one another, and pray for one another, that you may be healed. The effective, fervent prayer of a righteous man avails much." James encourages us to confess openly our failures so that prayer and healing can take place in our lives. Scott and I make it a habit to apologize to God, to each other and to our children when we argue in front of them. We take the time to explain to them where we went wrong, where we strayed from walking in love. We tell them that 1 John says, if we confess our sins, God is faithful and just to forgive us and cleanse us. We demonstrate repentance prayers to our children so that they can learn how to be like Peter. We want them to jump out of the boat and swim to Jesus whenever they fail. We want them to run into His loving embrace instead of away from it. We have experienced His correction and His goodness and we know He will never cast us out.

Create in me a clean heart, O God,
And renew a steadfast spirit within me.
11 Do not cast me away from Your presence,
And do not take Your Holy Spirit from me.

12 Restore to me the joy of Your salvation,
And uphold me by Your generous Spirit.
13 Then I will teach transgressors Your ways,
And sinners shall be converted to You.

Psalm 51:10-13 (NKJV)

THE POWER OF PUTTING YOUR MARRIAGE FIRST

Scott and I are busy people. We have six children and we are involved in our church and schools. I love to be an active member of my community. I enjoy community service and as a music teacher, I have the opportunity to interface with many people in my city, both parents, children, teachers and administrators. We attend a medium sized church that has opened many opportunities for ministry, including teaching engagements. If I chose, I could be away from my home every evening. I could choose to invest my time in arenas where I would be highly appreciated and I would experience great personal satisfaction. Over the last few years, however, God has been whittling down my activities outside of my home. When I find out about a new opportunity, I hear His voice ask me important questions, "Why do you want to do this? What will you have to give up if you do this? Will you be sacrificing time with Scott or your children?" The Holy Spirit has asked me to be extremely choosy about the activities that fill my life, because He has commanded me to put my marriage and children before any other ministry.

For the sake of transparency, I need to share that this is another area where I have struggled greatly, and God has faithfully changed the heart and mind. In times when things have been less than fulfilling at home, I have found it easier to work with voice students than to teach my own children to sing. I have found it more exciting to spend time in Bible studies at church than at home with my husband. At home, I am surrounded by familiarity: people who know my every flaw and often point them out to me. But at church and school, I still have some people fooled. In this season of my life, God is revealing to me the ultimate prize of a home full of His presence and love. This environment needs a special ingredient, and that ingredient is me.

Home is Scott's everyday life, and the focus of his ministry. When we took in our third son, Scott chose to quit his job and invest full-time in the children God was giving us. He gave up what would be considered "man's work" to do something so much more important: to father a generation. Before our third son came to live with us, Scott often used work as an escape from the difficult moments at home. He found fulfillment in providing financial support to his family, and when things were stressful in our marriage, he could release the pressure by working hard at his job. Since he is now a stay at home parent, he does not necessarily have that outlet. I make our marriage a priority by giving him opportunities to get out of the house and invest in himself. Scott is a body builder and enjoys exercise and spending time at the gym is extremely important for him. Scott loves to hunt and fish. I make sure that he has plenty of opportunities to go hunting and fishing with friends and by himself. Scott is the kind of man who meets God in his fishing boat, and I support his love the outdoors as an outlet for stress and an expression of his unique personality.

Scott makes our marriage a priority by speaking my love language on a regular basis. At the beginning of our marriage, Scott struggled with purchasing presents for me because of his frugal nature. At first, he only spoke my love language on Christmas and my birthday. He did not comprehend that the love language of gifts is no different than any other love language. I tried to explain to him that speaking it twice a year would never be acceptable, because I have a love tank that needs to be filled. It is no different than his love language of words of affirmation. It would never do for me to say uplifting things to him only on Christmas and his birthday. That would leave him feeling empty. He needs my daily prophetic voice released over his life. In the same way, I need him to regularly purchase something for me that is meaningful. He has learned to purchase me gifts regularly, and he gestures mean the world to me.

Scott and I choose to put our marriage before our children. Do not misunderstand me, our children are extremely important and we love them with all of our hearts. We make a concerted effort, however, to not allow them to dominate our lives. Our children are not the reason Scott and I are together. Their academics, activities, and social lives to do not dictate our every waking moment. We are married because God has called us to an eternal covenant with one another, and we make that covenant the centerpiece of our home, with Jesus on the throne. Our children know that even though they are loved and belong, their needs do not supersede the needs of our relationship. A good example of this is how we discipline our children. Our children know that their dad and mom will always agree on discipline. If Scott says no to something, Mom is in agreement. If I give out a consequence for disobedience, Dad is always on my side. Earlier this evening, I was sitting in my room for a moment, when I heard our oldest daughter backtalk Scott. Scott told her to go to her room and think about ways she could show respect in the future. When I came out, my daughter had come out of her room. She walked directly up to me and said, "Mom, I…"

"Hold it right there, Dear. You were disrespectful to your father a few minutes ago, correct?" I asked her.

"Yes," she replied.

"Thank you for telling me the truth. Did you apologize to your dad?" I asked.

"No." You could hear in her voice she knew what I was about to say.

"Well then," I said, "I need you to go and repent to your father before you speak to me." She chose not to repent and headed straight back to her room. A few minutes later, she came out and apologized to her father. I explained to her, "Your father matters to me more than anyone. If you disrespect him, please do not come and talk to me as if we are friends. Dad is my best friend, and my relationship to you will reflect how much respect you show him." She nodded and proceeded to do the chore he had originally asked her to do. In my eyes, this is the greatest win.

My daughter knows that my honor for Scott is a driving force in our home that cannot be hampered by her opinions or actions. It is outside of her control. Children want to know that grown-up things are in the hands of grown-ups and do not need to be managed by them. They feel safe when they know their parents are in charge and they, the children, can be children. Children of trauma have had to exert huge amounts of control in their lives. They have had to protect themselves from cruel treatment. Many of them have had to feed and clothe themselves at very young ages. When a child who has experienced this chaos comes into a home with both a father and a mother who love each other independent of their children, a home where adults are adults and children are children, they breathe a sigh of relief. They may continue with survival-like behaviors for a time. With each passing day, however, as they experience a marriage that is safe and loving, they will develop the freedom to let go of the control and manipulation they needed in their past lives.

Everything that Scott and I do is meant to bring healing to our children. We know that exposing our kids to the God-prescribed formula for marriage is not only good for us, it is also good for our kids. Our marriage has the potential to teach our children how to experience healthy intimacy, first with God, then with their future spouse. Just as Scott and I learned how to be spouses and parents from our own parents, we want to pass on to our children the wisdom that God has imparted to us. And we do not do this work alone. We surround our children with other powerful marriages that can build a compass within them that will not lead them astray. Our friends and family reinforce the truths we are teaching our children: That marriages are meant to reflect God's nature and character, that fathers and mothers are meant to live in harmony with one another, and that adults are called to demonstrate safe and loving behaviors to the next generation.

THE POWER OF INTIMACY

Marriage was instituted by God in the Garden of Eden, before sin had entered the picture. God created marriage to reflect the unity that He carries within Himself—within the Father, Son and Holy Spirit. Marriage was God's response to His statement, "It is not good for man to be alone." God knew that outside of intimate relationship, Adam could not fully reflect God's nature and character. I want to suggest that intimacy was the first act of worship in the Garden. It glorifies God when a man and woman experience oneness in the same fashion the Father experiences oneness with the Son and the Holy Spirit. What glorifies the Father is the truest act of worship. There was no need for sacrifice because there was no sin. But there WAS a need for intimacy. Intimacy is necessary for humans to be the image-bearers of God. Because of this, our enemy tries to destroy our intimacy with others. Satan spent millions of years in the presence of the Triune God, experiencing His fathomless glory and living within the beauty of God's unity and love. He understands the power of unity. Unity is the place where the anointing oil removes every burden and destroys every yoke. Unity is the place where eternal life manifests.

Behold, how good and how pleasant it is
For brethren to dwell together in unity!
It is like the precious oil upon the head,
Running down on the beard,
The beard of Aaron,
Running down on the edge of his garments.
It is like the dew of Hermon,
Descending upon the mountains of Zion;
For there the Lord commanded the blessing—
Life forevermore.

Psalm 133 (NKJV)

God intends for our unity to cause Jesus to manifest on the earth. Jesus, the Anointed One, finds a home in places of great unity. Jesus manifests in and through His Bride when she walks in unity with Him, each member fulfilling their created purpose in a unique way. Our enemy's great strategy is to drive the wedge of offense between husbands and wives, and between members of the Body of Christ, so that unity cannot bring forth the manifest presence of the Messiah.

Our marriages are God's priority, because the church is supposed to be built on the foundation of the family, not the other way around. God did not originally create an organization with governing bodies, rules and regulations, traditions and cultures. He created the family before the fall of man. Family is His original design, and family must be the focus of restoration ministry. The church is called to reflect the family dynamic, as the family reflects God's familial nature. What does that mean for our marriages? That means, intimacy between husband and wife is the most important ingredient to seeing the Kingdom of God spread on the earth. When that intimacy is broken, the family is divided and the church reflects this division. I believe if the church spent time healing the family, we would see far less church splits. I believe that if Husbands and wives made their marriage their primary calling, their children would reflect that unity and our churches would be full of fathered generation.

Scott and I have experienced the most powerful moments and also the most stressful moments of our relationship in the privacy of our bedroom. We have come to recognize that Satan despises spiritual, emotional and physical intimacy between a husband and wife, and he is doing everything in his power to keep us apart. He hates this intimacy for the very reason that in those moments of unity we reflect our Father most accurately. We get to be what Lucifer always wanted to be—like God. The number one tool that he uses to divide us is offense. If we open the door of offense in our hearts, our enemy will walk right in and take up residence. He stirs up unimportant irritations and frustrations that keep us from reaching out to one another. He hinders our communication so that we misunderstand each other. If the door of offense stays open, words start to fly out of our mouths that reflect his thoughts, not God's thoughts. Those words are seeds that are planted and can produce a very unhelpful harvest of bitterness and strife. Scott and I are endeavoring to be purposeful in confronting offense and speaking the opposite of what offense would dictate. Part of that process is admitting when we are offended and asking for forgiveness when we cause offense. It is the very opposite of what our enemy wants when we humble ourselves and reestablish connection with our covenant partner.

Dealing with offense can be a painful process. You might think that there is too much broken intimacy between you and your spouse to heal the wounds. That idea limits God's power to do a miracle in your life. Each of us needs to consider what we want for ourselves and what we desire for our children. Our kids are learning how to be married from us. Our choices either reflect God or they agree with the messages that our kids are already receiving from the world. Which would we choose for their future marriages? God is calling us to establish His Kingdom on the earth. That looks like intimacy and unity between husbands and wives. It looks like family units loving and serving one another. You are the primary source of instruction for your children and they will reflect you, whether they like it or not. What portrait would you like to see painted of yourself when your children are grown? Scott and I have decided, we want to see the very face of Jesus in our children, and we work hard to make our current intimate life the format.

Our children already know what broken intimacy looks like. They already know what it looks like when a man breaks a woman's body with his own hands. They know what it sounds like what moms and dads scream obscenities at each other and smash the personal belongings of the other into pieces. They know what it feels like when an adult forces them to meet his or her perverse needs. Satan has already used adults to build a perverted and horrific picture of intimacy. He is trying to ensure this next generation never experiences the beauty of God-prescribed intimacy between a husband and wife. We are called to be the intervention these children need. We are called to rescue them out of these disgusting circumstances and show them what is possible when Jesus is the King of our homes and hearts. We are privileged to show our children who this King of Glory really is. Because He is nothing like the human filth they have encountered so far. The beginning of this restoration is in our marriages.

They need to see dads and moms who hold hands and kiss in the kitchen. They need to see public displays of affection and connection. They have seen enough public displays of anger and abuse to last them a lifetime. Is this the best we can do for our kids? No, it is not. We need to remove from secrecy to transparency. Children need to know that intimacy between a husband and wife is sacred and private and special. They also need to know it is good to ask questions about intimacy and they need to know that they will receive answers to their questions. If they do not receive answers from their parents, they will certainly seek the answers somewhere else, and will receive information that does not agree with God's prescribed formula for intimacy. We must be the voice they hear in their minds, and what we speak and demonstrate needs to align with God's heart.

A STRONG MARRIAGE MEANS A STRONG FUTURE FOR YOUR CHILDREN

In the end, your children will thank you for loving your spouse well. They will thank you for teaching them how to walk in harmony with someone who is so different than them. They will be grateful that they learned from you the beauty of failure, because they will experience so many inevitable failures on their life journey. They will know that they can come to you, instead of to the world, to ask questions about intimacy. They will live more transparent and vulnerable lives because they learned it is safe to do so by watching you. Because of what they saw in your home, your children will seek relationships, both friendships, work partnerships and marriages, that imitate the Heavenly Family. They will want the kind of peace in their homes that they experienced in yours, and they will provide the safe boundaries for their children that you provided for them.

Perhaps the training you received from your parents was less than ideal. Perhaps you experienced some of the pain that my children have experienced and you are wondering whether there is still time to undo some of the patterns you have established in your home. The answer to that question is: there is always time in Christ. He has the supernatural ability to restore the years that the locusts have eaten. His purpose is to redeem your brokenness and restore your generations. Today is the day of new beginnings for you and your family, if you will only choose to start new with the power of the Holy Spirit. Perhaps you are a young adult who is considering starting a family through foster and adoption. You look at your growing up years and wonder if the patterns you see there will help you succeed or not. The truth is, in every family there are excellent, godly patterns and there are issues we would rather not repeat. This is true in every family. You have not only been fathered in the natural, however. You have also been fathered by God Himself. He can reveal to you a new way of doing things. With his assistance, your marriage can be just what this next generation of fatherless children needs. Trust Him to do in you what only He can do, and you will see great fruit in your life and in the lives of the children you love.

CHAPTER 6

Prophetic Parenting

What are the first words you can remember hearing your parents speak over you? I can tell you exactly what my mother sounds like when she tells me she loves me. She has been doing so every day of my life, since my first day on earth, and her voice has left an indelible mark on my brain. When I think back to my early years, I have emotional impressions about what my parents felt toward me. These impressions came from our interactions and the words they spoke about me. When I look back and put myself in the mind of a very small Harmony, I immediately feel love. I feel joy and the excitement of living. As a small girl, I know that I belong to my family and I am important in my family structure. I feel seen. There is, however, also an inner conflict that is present. I feel the knowledge that I am loved and wanted warring with a lie. The lie that is present is that I am a difficult and exasperating child. I feel a sense of abandonment because of the absence of my biological father. Even though I am surrounded by love, internally I wonder, "But, why doesn't *he* love me?" Both my feelings of love and belonging and the impression that there is something unlovable about me spring from my relationships with my parents. Although the overwhelming message of my childhood was that I was deeply loved, the abandonment of my biological father left wounds in my soul that manifested as anger, rejection and fear. My parents who were present and invested in my life used their powerful voices to speak truth over me, even in the face of a hyper-emotional child. Over the course of my life, the fruit of my parent's voices has been revealed, and the fruit is abundant and good. Even though some mixed messages may have gotten through, as an adult I have chosen to partner with the prophetic voice of God in my life to see what my parents envisioned about me come to pass.

This is the reality that all parents face. We are imperfect, flawed human beings and our flaws impact our children. If that was the extent of who we are there would be no hope. Yet there is hope, because God has fathered us, and has given us the power to reflect Him to our children. He has given us the authority to sow His Word into the fertile soil of our children's hearts and see that Word bear fruit. As my parents have seen in the course of their six children's lives, their godly influence has produced adults who love God and love their families. These six adults are not the product of chance. They are the product of prophetic parents who knew their words carried weight. We are a living, supernatural IRA account that our parents have diligently stashed sums in for a future date. And God Himself is making the withdrawals. We are a garden that my parents have cultivated, and God Himself is using the produce to feed the world.

What conversation with your parent has stayed with you the longest? The most poignant conversations I had with my father growing up were in moments where I was hungering for identity and he released God's perspective over me. These important conversations took place in the most mundane junctures of my life. They were not at graduations or important family functions. Instead, they took place in the car when he picked me up from swim team practice or when we were clothes shopping together. They left a huge impact on my mind and heart, not because the moment was important, but because the words were prophetic. When my father told me that I should wear the clothes I liked and felt comfortable in instead of trying to dress to please my peers, it gave me voice and choice. Before that moment, I felt under the control of other's opinions, and I had no idea how to get free from it. With one sentence, he changed my mindset and gave me freedom to express my own unique, God-given personality. When my father told me that I should run in my lane by pursuing music and drama, instead of trying to do activities that I thought would make me popular, I received from him the knowledge that I am who God designed me to be. I began to believe that I was good enough, just as God made me. When I was 11, my mother put a book in my hands. It was *A Wrinkle in Time* by Madeleine L'Engle. She said to me, "The little girl in this book has the same gifting as you. She is a namer, which means she reveals to people their true identity. You are called to prophesy, to tell people what God says about them." I read the book and internalized the words my mother released over my life. God had anointed me to prophesy, and at a very young age I began to do so.

It was natural for me to believe what my parents said about me. This is true for all children. If a child is told by her parents on a regular basis that she is loved, then she will reflect that reality. If she is told she is a problem, she will reflect that lie. In the impressionable mind of a child, it does not matter whether the words are true or not, it matters who speaks them and how often they are uttered. The authority and presence of the parent gives them a status in their children's lives that others do not have. That status is the same status that God told Moses he possessed.

Now you shall speak to [Aaron] and put the words in his mouth. And I will be with your mouth and with his mouth, and I will teach you what you shall do. So he shall be your spokesman to the people. And he himself shall be as a mouth for you, and you shall be to him as God.

Exodus 4:15-16 (NKJV)

There is only one God, but he has called us to be His spokesperson to our children and to the world. It is cliché, but it is also true that you may be the only Jesus your children see. What are we showing them? How are we using our voices to shape their worlds? In this chapter we will discuss how God has used Scott's and my prophetic voice in our children's lives and how each of us is called to prophesy over our children's lives until God's Word becomes our waking reality.

PROPHETIC PARENTS FROM SCRIPTURE

God is the prophetic Voice that all of creation obeys. His nature is a prophetic nature. When He speaks all the atoms and molecules of creation rush to obey what He has said. We see in the first chapter of Genesis that the Trinity only needed to be present and speaking for creation to manifest. His Word and His Spirit worked together to make what is invisible (the words of God) visible. Before the Trinity formed man from the clay of the earth, He released man's destiny with His voice:

Then God said, "Let Us make man in Our image, according to Our likeness; let them have dominion over the fish of the sea, over the birds of the air, and over the cattle, over all the earth and over every creeping thing that creeps on the earth." So God created man in His own image; in the image of God He created him; male and female He created them.

Genesis 1:26-27 (NKJV)

There was no doubt in God's mind that His words would become a reality, because He exalts His Word even above His name. He has given all power and all authority to His Word, and that power and authority has been established upon the earth through Jesus. God has never ceased to speak and create.

That would be counter-intuitive to His nature, which we know from Scripture does not change. We are the living expression of His Word, and we are called to speak His Word and watch as His creative power is released in the earth.

I lifted my eyes and looked, and behold, a certain man clothed in linen, whose waist was girded with gold of Uphaz! His body was like beryl, his face like the appearance of lightning, his eyes like torches of fire, his arms and feet like burnished bronze in color, and the sound of his words like the voice of a multitude.

Daniel 10:5-6 (NKJV)

The sound of His voice is like the voice of a multitude releasing His will into the earth. His sound is the prophetic voice of His sons and daughters. The Scripture exists because of the unity that God brought between His voice and the voices of His Children throughout history. This unity is a purpose of heaven that continues to take place each time we submit to the Holy Spirit and allow Him to speak through us.

God is calling to the parents of the Kingdom to arise in their identity as prophetic voices. We see examples of this type of parenting throughout the Scripture. It was an important part of the Jewish culture that fathers would lay hands on their children and release over them words of blessing. Although there is no record of how this tradition began, the first instance we see of it in the Scripture is God Himself, the Father of all humans, in the book of Genesis. He commands Adam and Eve to be fruitful and multiply and to have dominion over all of creation. Thus, we can gather that the tradition of blessing comes from our Heavenly Father's nature, not merely from human whim.

The second instance we find of a spoken blessing is Noah initiating blessings and curses over his sons after the incident of Noah's drunkenness. Noah made wine from his crop of grapes and became intoxicated. His son Canaan found him naked, and instead of protecting his father's dignity, ran to his brothers and exposed his father to them. They decided to honor Noah, even though he had clearly made a mistake. They carried a blanket between themselves, and walked backward until they had covered Noah's nakedness. On a side note, this is such a beautiful return of the blessing and protection that parents offer to their children. Noah had rescued his entire family from the flood by obeying God and building the ark. They returned the favor by honoring their father and covering his nakedness. In the light of what Noah did for his family, Canaan's betrayal becomes even more disrespectful and unnecessary. Noah was grateful for his sons who protected him when he was most vulnerable and blessed them with the name of the Lord. He then spoke a curse over his son Canaan, which was a seed of destruction that would haunt Canaan's descendants for generations. The descendants of Canaan were defeated and obliterated by the Israelite army when they crossed the Jordan with Joshua. Shem, on the other hand, passed down a worshiping blessing to his sons because he chose to protect and honor his father.

And he said: "Blessed be the LORD, The God of Shem, And may Canaan be his servant. May God enlarge Japheth, And may he dwell in the tents of Shem; And may Canaan be his servant."

Nine generations after Shem lived, Abram came on the scene. God reached out to Abram, although he had never offered a single sacrifice, never uttered a prayer to the Lord. As I sat reading again the story of Abram in preparation for this chapter, I asked the Lord, "Holy Spirit, why did you choose him? When You chose Noah, You Word says he was righteous in his generation. But there is no evidence that Abram was anyone special." The Holy Spirit reminded me of Noah's blessing over the line of Shem. "I honor the prophetic, creative voice of My children," the Holy Spirit responded to me. "It is My nature and character operating in them, and I honor My Word in their mouths." God chose Abram because he was a direct descendant of Shem, the one whom Noah said worshipped the Lord. The statement, "The God of Shem," is a statement of ownership. It is small phrase that packs a big punch. It indicates that Shem had a personal relationship with the Lord. It means that Shem chose to worship YHWH, instead of any of the pagan gods around him. He becomes the carrier of the worshiping blessing which God Himself awakens within Abram in Genesis chapter 12.

Now the Lord had said to Abram:
"Get out of your country,
From your family
And from your father's house,
To a land that I will show you.
I will make you a great nation;
I will bless you
And make your name great;
And you shall be a blessing.
I will bless those who bless you,
And I will curse him who curses you;
And in you all the families of the earth shall be blessed."

Genesis 12:1-3

God reveals Himself to Abram in the role of the Father who blesses. This would have been evident to Abram, who was born into a culture that prized spoken blessings. Abram would have recognized God's Words as both a covenant and a blessing. Abram understood that he too had a job to do. He needed to get out of his earthly father's country in order to experience his Heavenly Father's blessing, a blessing that would be perpetuated in his children's children to a thousand generations.

God's fatherly blessing is reiterated in the meeting of Melchizedek and Abram. Melchizedek, the priest of the Lord, speaks blessing over Abram.

Then Melchizedek king of Salem brought out bread and wine; he was the priest of God Most High. And he blessed him and said: "Blessed be Abram of God Most High, possessor of heaven and earth; and blessed be God Most High, who has delivered your enemies into your hand." And he gave him a tithe of all.

Genesis 14:18-20

I believe God sent Melchizedek to remind Abram of God's original blessing. God is saying to Abram, "Remember what I promised would happen if you obeyed me? You did, and here is your reward." Like Noah, Melchizedek blesses Abram with the name of the Lord. It is a worshiping blessing that Abram receives. And it is not just a blessing that belongs to him, but to his children as well. The question is, will he recognize that he can pass this blessing on to his children or not?

It is important to recognize that God is the Initiator of blessing. He is the starting place for all creative power. His Word goes out from His mouth to accomplish His purposes, and we have an opportunity to become part of that unstoppable process. Our mouths were designed to partner with God's creative power, as Adam's did when he named the animals and as Noah's did when he blessed Shem. We can either join the party or leave the that part of our nature dormant. God's love is so great, however, that He often comes and wakes us up with His own voice. He desires that His children would reflect Him to the extent that, when a father's prophetic voice is missing, He

Himself will speak from heaven, or send another to speak on His behalf. That is His fathering heart and His loving nature. If we choose, however, we can actively step into the pattern of prophetic parenting that God left us in His Word.

God's blessing over Abram and his family was powerful enough in itself, but God was not done shaping Abram with His Words. The Father renames Abram to Abraham, inserting His fathering nature into his name. The Lord expands Abram's destiny through His prophetic blessing, and He expands Abram's name to encompass that greatness of that calling. The name Abram means "high father"[1]. I imagine that at times this name stung Abram's heart. There must have been many moments where he found the irony of his name a bitter pill to chew. Yet God expands the power and importance of Abrams name. He changes the contraction from "father-high" to "father of a multitude"[2]. Destiny is laced through every aspect of God's prophetic name for his earthly son.

Although Abraham experienced the power of God's blessing, there is no record of him releasing that blessing over his son. There is, however, a record of Isaac and Abraham worshiping together. God asked Abraham to sacrifice his beloved son Isaac on the altar, and Abraham did not withhold his son from the Lord. He believed that God would provide for Himself a lamb and that God would keep His promises. He taught his son to worship God, even when it may cost him the thing he loves the most. He taught Isaac to trust God in the midst of unthinkable circumstances, and Isaac was present when the audible voice of God spoke to his father from heaven. Because of Abraham's obedience, his son had face-to-face encounters

---

1   James Strong, The New Strong's Expanded Exhaustive Concordance of The Bible: Hebrew and Aramaic Dictionary, (Nashville, Thomas Nelson Publishers, 2001), 4.

2   James Strong, The New Strong's Expanded Exhaustive Concordance of The Bible: Hebrew and Aramaic Dictionary, (Nashville, Thomas Nelson Publishers, 2001), 4.

with God's voice. When Abraham was about to die, Genesis 25 says that he gave all that he had to his son Isaac. He did not just pass on his material wealth to his son. He also passed on the blessing of God's presence and favor. After the death of Abraham, God Himself visited Isaac and blessed him. God's voice and God's presence was normal for Isaac. He learned to hear and abide from his father Abraham.

What kind of "normal" are we creating for our children? I ask myself this often, because I want God's voice to be an everyday occurrence in their lives. I want Brenden's testimony of knowing what God has to say about him to be the experience of every person who walks through my door. The best way to train our children to know Him intimately is to make Him as common in our homes as bathing and eating. Our children catch our focuses and passions. They pick up on what matters to us and those priorities become theirs. Just as my father's most impactful moments with me happened on normal, seemingly unimportant days, the inclusion of God's presence and love in the little moments of our day form a child's mindsets and emotions.

Although Isaac knew God's presence and His blessing, he did not develop an environment of worship for his family. There seems to be division in Isaac's household that centers on the parents' favoritism. Rebekah loved Jacob, but Isaac preferred his son Esau. Instead of giving us the detailed account of Isaac's triumphs and failures, the storyteller jumps directly from the twins' birth into the rivalry that existed between Jacob and his older twin when they were adults. Even though God speaks directly to Isaac in Genesis 26 and repeats His promise to Abraham, Isaac does not teach his sons to hear God's voice. Instead of imitating his father's habits of worship, he imitated his father's sin by pretending his wife was his sister, as Abraham had done when he visited Egypt. Instead of stepping up and blessing both of his sons, releasing a unique, God-ordained destiny over each of them, Isaac leaves his sons to bicker with little to no input from him. Left to his own devices, Jacob manifests the meaning of his name (Jacob means "supplanter"), and tricks his brother into giving Jacob his birthright. Instead of believing that God would fulfill His promises to her sons, Rebekah encourages Jacob to steal his father's blessing through deceit.

This family is missing the mark because they do not recognize their ability to reflect God's nature and character. Isaac did not realize that he could have blessed each of his sons without detracting from the blessing of the other. He forgot that his father's name had been expanded to fit a larger capacity to birth sons. He forgot that God had promised that through Isaac *all* of the nations of the earth would be blessed. God's blessing has no limits, but Isaac had forgotten to reflect the fathering nature of the Lord. When Jacob becomes a father, he seeks to redeem the brokenness that he experienced in his father's home. He chooses to speak both blessings and curses over all of his sons, calling out their strengths and disciplining them for their sin, as well. The last chapter of Genesis is a powerful picture of the prophetic voice every father is meant to have in the lives of his children.

RELEASING IDENTITY

Jacob longed to be fathered. He longed to be claimed and to be acknowledged as an important member of his family. Jacob was willing to go to any lengths to receive a father's blessing, even if that meant lying and cheating. I have known children like this. More than anything, they want to belong. They want to know that their lives have meaning and that someone will claim them, even in their brokenness. They are crying out to be defined by the One who designed them. They look to us to find out what the Heavenly Father looks and sounds like. They will judge God, often unfairly, based on what they see in their parents. We are called to be the doorway for prophetic identity to be released into the lives of our children. It is our job to find the gold that is hiding under layers of rock and dirt. Our job is to dig deeply into our children and uncover what God has planted within them.

My foster and adoptive children echo the story of Esau and Jacob. They hold tight to us, doing everything in their power to get our attention. They wish only to be the apple of our eye. They wish to be favored. When they see others receive favor and blessing, they become envious and spiteful. They weep like Esau and cry, "Bless me, too, Father!" They do not know that the blessing of another can never subtract from what God has planned for them. Their actions may be self-destructive or disobedient, but they have a purpose. That purpose is to capture our vision. Before our children came to us, they were often ignored by the adults in their lives. They were left to fend for themselves, to find their own food and look out for themselves at home when parents were away. Like Esau and Jacob, they were left to their own devices and did the best they could to navigate a scary world, without proper boundaries or safety nets. They developed habits that made sense for a person surviving, but that do not agree with their God-given identity in any way. Now, they are among safe adults and they are wrestling to be blessed. They are crying out, "I won't let you go until you bless me." They are listening for a voice that can see past the exterior rebellion to the beauty within.

Two key ingredients to releasing identity in our children's lives are presence and prophecy. To our children, love is spelled "T-I-M-E". Our mere presence creates a sense of safety for our kids. When we have meaningful, face-to-face conversations with them, where they can look us in the eye and read our expressions and body language, they begin to pick up on our hearts for them. They learn to laugh and experience freedom in our presence. When we spend time with our children, there are many moments to offer affection to them, to reach out and connect with them through hugs, high-fives and a hand on the shoulder. This affection creates bonds of trust between us and our children and it opens the lines of communication. Time and affection are the currency which we deposit into our kids, and these deposits have an astounding affect on the way they think, speak and act. Even a child who has experienced horrible abuse and neglect can learn to trust again and to think differently about themselves and others. This transformation happens as parents invest presence into children. Also, presence means safety. Left to their own devices, children will use their irrational brains to get themselves into trouble. They can quickly hurt themselves or others if there is no one there to intervene. My presence is a reminder to my children that there is a boundary, both visible (me) and invisible (Holy Spirit), that keeps them from making unsafe choices.

After we have established ourselves in our children's lives through time and affection, their hearts begin to trust us. Words have proven false to our kids throughout their short lives. Parents promise to visit them, but never show up for a visit. Parents promise never to hit them again, but continue to physically abuse them. They have learned through the behaviors of the adults around them that actions speak louder than words. Simultaneously, these same children have learned to wear the words of their biological families like badges. They parrot the abusive words that have been flung on them. They label others in the same way they have been labeled. How do we counteract this cycle? We remember that we carry God's creative voice within us.

And when the disciples saw it, they marveled, saying, "How did the fig tree wither away so soon?" So Jesus answered and said to them, "Assuredly, I say to you, if you have faith and do not doubt, you will not only do what was done to the fig tree, but also if you say to this mountain, 'Be removed and be cast into the sea,' it will be done. And whatever things you ask in prayer, believing, you will receive."

Matthew 21:20-22

This passage is repeated three times in the synoptic gospels - twice in Matthew and once in Mark. This is a faith mandate given us by Jesus. His disciples were astonished that when Jesus commanded the fig tree to wither, it did so and quickly. Jesus' response to them is to remind them that they too carry the creative power of God's voice. He reminds them that He is the prototype after which all of God's children are to be fashioned. He is the Firstborn of many brothers and sisters. In fact, Jesus promises us that those who believe in Him will do even greater works than He performed while on earth (John 14:12). In the lives of our children, we will see the creative fruit of our words, even if we choose to sow unwittingly into them. Their hearts are fertile soil, and our words are the seeds. We get to decide to purposefully sow the living Word of God into our children, and see the fruit of those words benefit our children and everyone around them.

UNLOCKING DESTINY

I have had the great privilege of mentoring the biological mother of my eight-year-old son. I have been witness to the transformation of this lady's life, as she has committed her life to Jesus, was baptized, went back to school, and graduated successfully. She went from living in a homeless shelter to having her own apartment where she is successfully raising one of her children. She has a full-time job now, and has been drug-free for more than three years. Mentoring biological family members is not the main focus of our ministry, but in the case of this Mom, I have had the opportunity to help her grow and mature and overcome her substance abuse. She shared an interesting perspective with me one day. "When I was growing up, I never heard the word 'college' mentioned. I didn't know that school was important. My mom doesn't have her license, I don't and my brother doesn't. None of us drive. That's just the way it is. When I went back to school, I never expected to succeed, because no one in my family ever had." Do you see a pattern in her speech? I do. The thread that runs through it is generational brokenness.

Fostering and adopting fatherless children means interrupting the generational iniquities that run in their biological families and unlocking the seeds of greatness that are lying dormant in their family lines. These seeds exist, not because of us, but because God has been faithfully planting His Word along the way. More seeds will be planted while these children are in our home that will partner with what already lies inside of them, but the framework is already there. The image of God is already written into their DNA. They only need a prophetic voice to unlock it. The amazing mother I spoke of earlier has become a member of our family. She recognizes that we are unlocking something powerful inside of her son that the enemy has tried to keep dead for many generations. And not only in her son, but also inside of her, lie these sleeping seeds. We are speaking to the dry bones in both of them: "Live."

This is the same power that Peter used when he commanded Tabitha to arise. Peter was there the day Jesus commanded the waves to be still. He was there when the fig tree withered and when Lazarus came out of the tomb at Jesus' command. He remembered the words of Christ, "If you believe in Me, you can also command the mountains to be moved and it will happen." Peter remembered his Lord commissioning them, "And these signs will follow those who believe: In My name they will cast out demons; they will speak with new tongues; they will take up serpents; and if they drink anything deadly, it will by no means hurt them; they will lay hands on the sick, and they will recover." (Mark 16:17-18) Each of us who believe are contained within the Great Commission. Put your own name in every place where the word "they" appears. In Jesus' name, *you* will cast out demons; *you* will speak with new tongues; *you* will lay hands on the sick and see them recover. You. This is exactly what a fatherless generation needs. They need those who believe to walk in the creative power of Jesus the Messiah.

With that creative power, we have seen children who did not speak in full sentences learn to communicate well. We have seen eligibilities for special needs programs fall off because the child no longer demonstrates the special need. We were not miracle workers, but we were filled with the Spirit of the Messiah, whose authority worked through our words. As our children experienced growth, they began to see that what Dad and Mom said about them was true. They could see the fruit for themselves and began to believe our prophetic words until those words became their own words. That is our goal, just as it was Jesus' goal; that our sons and daughters would believe they are image-bearers of God Almighty and speak and act according to the divine nature which lives inside of them.

For God, who said, "Let brilliant light shine out of darkness," is the one who has cascaded his light into us—the brilliant dawning light of the glorious knowledge of God as we gaze into the face of Jesus Christ. We are like common clay jars that carry this glorious treasure within, so that the extraordinary overflow of power will be seen as God's, not ours.

2 Corinthians 4:6-7

AFTER HIS IMAGE

Each human that has ever walked upon the earth was here because God ordained it. He wrote within each one a supernatural design and purpose. There are no accidents, no mistakes, when it comes to the entry of each human soul into time and space. God intends for us to discover what He Himself has written in our inner persons. He has called us to manifest his glory and to water the seeds that lie within others. It is a thrill to watch God's nature and character break through the soil of a child's heart. There is nothing more satisfying than to see a son or daughter recognize their own potential. When that young person begins to partner with God and speak prophetically over his or her own life, that is when we realize there is nothing more valuable than teaching a child to hear and believe God's voice.

I have heard many preachers say, there is no junior Holy Spirit. The same power that adults carry to prophesy over other's lives is the power that is sleeping inside our children. Think of Samuel. His mother, Hannah, cried out to God because of her barrenness, and God heard her prayers. He opened her womb and she conceived. When Samuel was weaned, Hannah took her firstborn son to the tabernacle of the Lord and gave him to the high priest Eli. She dedicated her child to the work of the Lord, and Samuel served the Lord and His high priest from that moment on. Think of the implications of this story. If Samuel were weaned at two or three years old, he would have no memories prior to his time in the tabernacle. Samuel's first visual memories would have been of the table of showbread in the Holy Place. His first aroma memories would have been of the incense offered to God in that most sacred space. His little ears would have been tuned to the prayers of the priests as they offered sacrifices to the Lord. His first words would perhaps have been a child-like imitation of those prayers. He ate the meat that was given to the priests as their portion. He was sanctified by the presence of the Most High God. It is not surprising then that at eleven years old (according to scholars), Samuel was sleeping in the Holy Place. Between him and the mercy seat stood only the veil. His subconscious and conscious mind have been formed by his encounters in God's dwelling place, and his mind was a place where God's voice would be welcome.

All of these factors preceded Samuel's face-to-face encounter with Yahweh. They preceded Samuel's commissioning as a prophet to God's people. His mother Hannah set Samuel up for spiritual success by positioning him in God's presence. This is the calling of parents everywhere. We have the unique privilege of creating an environment for our children where encounters with God are the new "normal". Although we cannot choose for our children what their first memories will be, we can inundate their young minds with voice of love and truth that calls out to God's image within them. We can prophesy over their lives and over our own lives, teaching them to do the same. Then it will not surprise us when our children tell us they have heard God's voice, as Samuel did, and as my son Brenden did.

CHAPTER 7

Overcoming "What If"

It is tempting to look at the enormity and depth of this problem and think to yourself, "I am not fit for such a task." It is easy to say to yourself, "I don't always hear God's voice for myself. How could I hear it for traumatized children?" I have had 14 foster children in the last three years, and there are days when I still say to myself, "I can't do this." Then I remind myself that we said yes and now must either submit to God or send our kids back to the state. Clearly, the second is not an option, which helps me come to the best conclusion. That does not mean, however, that voices do not arise who tell me I am no good at what I do, that I should throw in the towel, that I should leave it in more capable hands. I am sure you can guess where these voices arise from, and it is not the presence of God. Read this paragraph again - everywhere you see quotations, you are reading the words of someone *other* than the Father.

Those voices arise from my flesh and from the source of all lies, Satan. (The word "satan" means "accuser.") I am not being overly dramatic, either. Satan hates innocence. He revels in its destruction. He enjoys watching children suffer and he does not want the cycles of abuse to be interrupted by Christ followers. First, he does his best to keep broken adults in their brokenness. He knows the same truth that God revealed in His Word; that the image of God in every child is either buried or revealed through the behaviors of parents. Second, he aims to keep abused children silent. He shames them for exposing their abusers, and increases the abuse when they finally find the courage to come forward. Third, he seeks to hinder all those who would step up to father and mother a broken generation. He hinders them through self-hatred, fear, and, the big killer of God's design for family: divorce. The enemy loves to disqualify the called by pointing out their areas of weakness (As if being imperfect could ever disqualify one whom God has called!). Once we have yielded to God's intention for the church to invade the kingdom of darkness and to rescue our children from its clutches, our enemy goes about destroying us in a different way. In a vain attempt to stop us from doing what we have set our faces to do, he pesters us with all the ways in which we could fail.

I am about to confront every one of Satan's insidious lies. I will present you with what God's Word teaches concerning our fears and concerns and I will share our personal experiences within the foster care system. You will find that Satan knows how to use the reality of this human, fallen world to scare Christians into never using the authority they carry. He wants us to be obsessed with the obstacles when we are called to obliterate them. Satan does not want us to recognize that we are seated in heavenly places at this moment, in Christ. He does not want our thinking and behavior to shift so that our natural reality begins to reflect the supernatural environment of Heaven. But *what if* we saw our families and communities the way that God has spoken them to be? *What if* the church reflected the heart of God in the manner it was meant to? That would not only silence the accuser, it would bring creation into obedience to God. This chapter is the removal of every excuse that could keep a man and woman of God from using the authority of Jesus to change the world.

WHAT IF I HAVE A PAST?

Listen to my testimony: I cried to God in my distress

and he answered me. He freed me from all my fears!
Gaze upon him, join your life with his, and joy will come.
Your faces will glisten with glory.
You'll never wear that shame-face again.
When I had nothing, desperate and defeated,
I cried out to the Lord and he heard me,
bringing his miracle-deliverance when I needed it most.

Psalm 34:4-6 (TPT)

This passage has always been important to me personally. After coming out of a cult and an abusive marriage, I was consumed with shame. I felt like I had squandered my talent and treasure for six years of my life. I felt like I had missed important opportunities. I felt like I would never accomplish the great things my grandparents and parents had dreamed for me. How could I be the woman whose husband beats her and is unfaithful to her? Even though my first husband's faults were his responsibility and not mine, I felt responsible and ashamed that I had allowed myself to be treated like that. My feelings were lying to me. They did not agree with what God said about me, but at the time I was so broken, I did not have the discernment to confront those lies. And, to be fair, when I first came out of such a terrible and painful situation, there was a lot of healing and restoration that God intended to do in my life before I was ready "change the world".

What I did not know at the time was that the process of healing would be a hug tool for ministering to my children in the future. What I did not know was that my testimony would give other women the courage to leave their abusers. I did not know ten years ago that one day I would be the mother of six children and wife to Scott. I did not know that he and I would be ministering to children with high needs that stem from trauma like I experienced in my first marriage. I did not know that the children we would raise would need the compassion and understanding that comes from walking a similar path. I did not know at the time that they would need a mother who can hold them and say, "I have felt what you are feeling. Let's invite Jesus to come in and heal those hurts." I did not know that ten years later, I would be writing a book where I would share our story and encourage others to join us in this work. But God knew and He never wasted one moment of my life. He was preparing me.

Our stories are the seeds of change that can take root in another's heart. Our stories have creative power to awaken the call within others. We are called to partner our testimonies with the blood of the Lamb to overcome the accuser, his strategies and his principalities.

Then I heard a loud voice saying in heaven, "Now salvation, and strength, and the kingdom of our God, and the power of His Christ have come, for the accuser of our brethren, who accused them before our God day and night, has been cast down. 11 And they overcame him by the blood of the Lamb and by the word of their testimony, and they did not love their lives to the death.

Revelation 12:10-11 (NKJV)

The enemy longs to silence you. He wants no remembrance of the faithfulness of God in your life. He hates the ebenezers we build to honor God's miraculous intervention, and he longs to stop up the chain breaking freedom within you that can set others free. Satan stands ready to accuse you. Satan will tell you that you are not smart enough or strong enough or spiritual enough to minister to others. He will tell you that "real" Christians will never respect you because of your past. "If they find out, he whispers, they will not want you around, and they certainly never allow you to minister to anyone." The very opposite is true. When we are open about what God has done in our lives, it offers hope to others. Our story tells others they are not alone in their darkness and that, if God can rescue one sinner and turn them into a son or daughter, then He can and *will* most certainly do it again.

Our children need to hear our stories. They need to know that there is hope for them in the midst of their mess and that Jesus is with them in the process. He loves them NOW, as they are, and not at some distant moment in the future. Who better to teach them this concept than those of us who have experienced the outpouring of His love that transforms a life? We *know* that God keeps His promises because we have experienced it. We can pass on this confidence to the next generation if we so choose. This next generation is in desperate need of the hope that we can give them, the hope we know firsthand.

Think of the woman at the well in John chapter four. Did her five broken marriages and her live-in boyfriend disqualify her from sharing Jesus' words with her village? Indeed, no! Many scholars believe that because of her familiarity with the men of the village, she was able to share the news that the Messiah had come freely, instead of being hindered by culturally accepted mores imposed on the women of that time. I am not implying here that the Father wanted her to have five husbands or an intimate relationship outside of marriage. God never intends for us to choose sin, nor does he enjoy our suffering. But when we sin and when we suffer, God has promised to use *all things* together for good for those who love Him and are called according to His purposes. The Father will not waste our trials. He will train us to trust Him through every challenge and give us opportunities to say to others, "I've been where you are. Let me tell you what God did for me." He will make victory over the enemy the new norm in our lives so that we can teach others to expect the victory, instead of defeat.

WHAT IF MY FOSTER CHILD HATES ME?

As I mentioned earlier in the book, foster children have been through excruciating circumstances. Even if they were being physically, sexually or verbally abused by their biological family, they are bonded to and devoted to the very people who hurt them the worst. When they are removed from their homes, everything that was valuable to them is lost. They feel personally responsible for the pain they are in. They do not put the blame and responsibility where it belongs, We should expect that these children will be offended by us on a regular basis. We live differently than their families and there is an implication that our way is better, which hurts our children. They feel the need to defend their biological parents, even when they know they are better off away from them. Although these children are crying out for a safe environment, for boundaries, discipline and affection, they often reject the very blessings they need because to do so would be disloyal to their abusers. It would be admitting that there is something wrong with what was done to them.

Children who have lost everything long for some control in their lives. They may refuse to eat. They may steal or destroy private property. Some run away from home. Some get into physical fights with peers or adults. It may seem hard to understand, but there are actually very strong motivators and biological processes that encourage children of trauma to exhibit behaviors that lead to more pain. Trauma and abuse change the way the child's brain functions[1]. The neuro-pathways in the brain of an abused child look different than a "typical" child's brain. Their normal responses will be based on their past need to survive and their fear of rejection and

---

[1]   United States. US Department of Health and Human Services. Washington, DC. Parenting a Child Who Has Experienced Trauma. Washington, D.C.

abandonment. It will take years to rewrite those pathways, and some of them will be a life long struggle that only Jesus can fully mend.

The question really is not *if* they will dislike you. Their emotions will swing wildly from day to day. There will be days when your foster child is so grateful for a warm bed and a filling meal and safe hug, and there will be days when they reject everything you offer them with no real substantial reason to do so. Children of trauma go through trauma seasons - days upon which they experienced such horrors that their subconscious regurgitates those experiences through flashbacks and nightmares. In the days leading up to the anniversary of the child, you may see behaviors crop up that have been sleeping for a while. Your child arriving in your home may be a happy memory for you, but for many of these children it is the season of their greatest pain. The abuse that prompted their removal from their biological family happened in those days and weeks. Their greatest loss - the loss of those same family members - happened on a day of joy for you. While you rejoice that they came to be a member of your family, they struggle, rebel, revert to old behaviors, because their hearts are broken. This is to be expected.

It is best to prepare for the worst while continually holding yourself and your child to the highest standard possible. When they reject you, which they will, remember what they have been through. Do the impossible and pour out on them what they least expect: unconditional love. Remember that you did not embark on this journey to be accepted by humans but to hear your Heavenly Father say, "Well done, good and faithful servant." Think of what Jesus endured because He was obedient to the Father. What we endure to love these children is not nearly so painful as a brutal death on the cross. He suffered for us and as us, and He will empower us to love those for whom He died.

Blessed are you when they revile and persecute you, and say all kinds of evil against you falsely for My sake. Rejoice and be exceedingly glad, for great is your reward in heaven, for so they persecuted the prophets who were before you.

Matthew 5:11-12 (NKJV)

Should a child's rejection of you stop you from giving them what only you can give? Should their brokenness be powerful enough to hinder your spiritual authority? There is a flaw in our self-view if we think the God within us is not big enough to love a broken child through us. He is big enough, but He is also a God of relationship and unity. He desires our buy-in, our decision to come into agreement with His eternal plans for the fatherless. He wants to use us as Jesus with skin on for a child who needs a face-to-face encounter with God's supernatural love.

WHAT IF MY CHILD DOESN'T CHANGE?

So then, from now on, we have a new perspective that refuses to evaluate people merely by their outward appearances. For that's how we once viewed the Anointed One, but no longer do we see him with limited human insight. Now, if anyone is enfolded into Christ, he has become an entirely new creation. All that is related to the old order has vanished. Behold, everything is fresh and new. And God has made all things new, and reconciled us to himself, and given us the ministry of reconciling others to God. In other words, it was through the Anointed One that God was shepherding the world, not even keeping records of their transgressions, and he has entrusted to us the ministry of opening the door of reconciliation to God.

2 Corinthians 5:16-19 (TPT)

Change is an inevitable part of human existence. Some changes come naturally as we grow and mature. Some changes are forced upon us through the harmful behaviors of others. Children in the foster care system have experienced these types of forced changes many times in their lives. The problem is, however, that they do not recognize that those changes came because of the abusive choices of others. They do not know what they could have been without the presence of abuse and neglect in their lives. Their altered way of thinking and processing their external world is normal for them, and they have no comprehension that there might be a different way of thinking or feeling. When they attend school, they begin to recognize that they are not the same as their peers. They do not make friends easily, or they do not excel at academics or sports. Because of the lifestyle choices of their parents, they are unable to take part in after school activities or have sleepovers with friends. They feel alienated and they act out to get the attention they crave. Their emotional outbursts are a release for the pressure that is building within them. That pressure is the dread that something is very wrong with them, but do cannot identify what it is.

As adults who want to help kids, we may have grandiose dreams of what their lives could be like under our loving mentorship. I certainly did and do have huge hopes for my children. But I have learned that my hope needs to be anchored in Christ and not in the day to day behaviors of my children, because there will be days when it looks like all hope is lost. In the natural it looks like no strategy of Heaven or earth is working to help a child in my home. After three years of loving a child, they can suddenly return to a behavior they have not done in years. There is discouragement that comes in those moments. I have learned however, that *everything* may seem hopeless, and yet there is an eternal hope that never fades.

So it is impossible for God to lie for we know that his

promise and his vow will never change! And now we have run into his heart to hide ourselves in his faithfulness. This is where we find his strength and comfort, for he empowers us to seize what has already been established ahead of time—an unshakeable hope! We have this certain hope like a strong, unbreakable anchor holding our souls to God himself. Our anchor of hope is fastened to the mercy seat which sits in the heavenly realm beyond the sacred threshold, and where Jesus, our forerunner, has gone in before us. He is now and forever our royal Priest like Melchizedek.

Hebrews 6:18-20 (TPT)

There is an assurance that comes from knowing that the Trinity will keep Their Word forever. That assurance has nothing to do with what we see in the natural. It is a higher law, a law that supersedes the natural law, because the natural law was first brought into being by the law of His creative word. His Word will always win out in the end. If that is true, then we are carrying a power that can transform even the most devastated child. A miraculous love flows in and through us. We are the ministers of the Gospel of reconciliation, and the victory of the cross and resurrection are on our side. What darkness can stand against us?

As with any wound, however, it takes time for healing to take place. Some things will shift quickly in a foster or adopted child, and some will take years. When Brenden first came to us, there were battles we chose not to fight at all, because we believed that we should pick and choose wisely. We wanted him to experience success and personal pride in his growth rather quickly, so that when he had to face the giants in his life, he would be able to with confidence. We praised him for every small step of growth, and we downplayed the importance of failures. We taught him that failure is an opportunity to learn and grow. This is the truth for every child. We must let go of some of our preconceived notions of success and allow each child to develop at their own speed. Enjoy the process and breathe through the difficult challenges, knowing that God's intention for both you and your child is victory.

WHAT IF MY FOSTER CHILD HURTS MY NATURAL CHILD?

This is a fear that many prospective foster parents face. I have had couples considering foster care say to me, "Well, we would only be willing to take young children. We don't want to run the risk of an older child hurting our biological children." If this is a mindset you are confronting, I would suggest to you that both natural siblings and foster siblings hurt and help each other in numerous ways. I would suggest to you that your natural children have much to learn from a child who has not been blessed to live in a home like yours all of their lives. I would suggest that dangerous and painful circumstances can happen to a child outside of our homes, online, at school or even at church, and that it is impossible to protect them from every opportunity for injury that children are faced with every day. We do our best and set healthy boundaries, but injuries still occur, whether we foster or not.

I would also encourage you to think of foster care as a family ministry. As I stated earlier, Christian children do not have a junior Holy Spirit. They have been given gifts and strengths and talents that can benefit a child who did not grow up in a Christian home. There is a 30-million-word gap between children of poverty and middle class children. Think of the language skills that will develop within a foster child because of the time they spend chatting with your kids. Think of the fruit of compassion, understanding, and inclusion that can be developed within both biological and foster children through play and through conflict resolution. Your natural children can be taught that the ministry your family does is so that other families can be transformed by the Gospel of Jesus Christ, and that they get to be an important part of that Gospel work, if they so choose.

WHAT IF MY CHILD GOES BACK?

This is the hardest factor for most couples considering foster care. I hear them say, "I just couldn't take it if I had to give a child up." I have to agree that this has been the most painful part of our work as foster and adoptive parents. This aspect is more egregious than the intrusive behavior of DHS workers. It is more painful than all the hateful words our children have flung at us over the years. We love each child that comes through our door, and we intend from the first moment that they would find a forever home with us. You may consider this foolish, or even worse, destructive. You may think we do not care about the biological families of our children. You would be wrong to think that. We mentor biological family members when we can and include them in our family holidays and functions. We want our children to feel whole. Therefore, we intentionally include conversations about the loving member of their families and we pray for them together. There is a very good reason to treat children like they belong to us right away, however.

Children of trauma assume that they do not belong. They assume that they will be rejected and abandoned, because that is what they have experienced. As long as they feel in their hearts that no one wants them, their behaviors will line up with that belief. When the narrative has shifted, however, from rejection to acceptance, we find our children begin to let their guards down. In the case of two of our children, each of them had been in six different houses during their time in foster care. It is typical for an unruly or dangerous child to be sent away. On the other hand, Scott and I decided long ago that, unless for the safety of the other children, we would never send a child away. That was an easy decision to make when we only had Brenden and we were longing to parent more children. But when one of our kids molested our dog, our convictions were tested. Would we love this child through their abusive behaviors? Could we forgive and teach that child how to care for God's creatures, both human and animal? Or would we throw in the towel, and send that child off to a seventh home? We would have just made the wounds deeper and harder to heal.

Instead, we chose to forgive and to teach our child safe and loving boundaries. That child has never repeated that behavior in our home. I am convinced that child was asking me, "Will you reject me as well?" We chose to embrace our child even closer when he sinned against us. We still do this. God does not run away from us when we make mistakes. He does not turn His face away from us because Jesus' blood has been applied to the mercy seat on our behalf. He pulls us deeply into His Fatherly love. He reminds us of our worth. He kisses us and restores us, as he did with the prodigal son. His pleasure is to draw all mankind to Himself. We make an effort to draw our children to us through love and forgiveness. This has been the tool that has done the most to transform our children from orphans to sons and daughters.

We establish belonging for the benefit of our children, even though we know that if they leave us, they will tear our hearts out and carry them away. This is sacrificial love that all parents show their children. One day, all children grow into adulthood and leave their parents' home. That is a tough process and can be painful. Like those parents who send their kids off to college, we believe that we have done an excellent job with our kids, preparing them to go on to their next assignment. We also believe that even though our children may be separated from us physically, there is no distance in the spirit.

We will always pray for them and love them from afar. We believe that in the time they have been with us, they have received an impartation, a seed that will grow and bear much fruit. We also pray that one day they will return to us in one capacity or another. We leave the details to the Father, but we hold onto the hope that we will see them again one day. This gives us the courage to say goodbye when it is necessary.

WHAT IF I FAIL?

Failure is a human condition that we all experience. You are not alone, friend. We learn the most about God's faithfulness and love when we are confronted with our own shortcomings. I believe that God has been preparing you to read this book. I am convinced that you have faced many a trial in your life that has prepared you for the work that our Father is calling us to: a work that will take His supernatural presence and grace. It will not be by your own strength that you and your family rescue broken children. It will be as a direct result of your submission to His Spirit.

So he answered and said to me:
"This is the word of the Lord to Zerubbabel:
'Not by might nor by power, but by My Spirit,'
Says the Lord of hosts.
7 'Who are you, O great mountain?
Before Zerubbabel you shall become a plain!
And he shall bring forth the capstone
With shouts of "Grace, grace to it!"'"

Zechariah 4:6-7 (NKJV)

What is standing before you will be like the mountain before Zerubbabel. Nothing could permanently hinder what God had ordained for His earthly son. Zerubbabel believed the prophetic word that God had commanded him to rebuild the temple, and he chose to bring his thinking into alignment with that crazy dream. He could have argued with God about his qualifications. He could have been like Moses, "Pick someone else! Anyone else!" Yet, even though Moses did not think himself worthy to be God's messenger, he missed what was in him that prepared him for his future. You may be looking at yourself and seeing the lack. Will you choose to argue with God's purpose, or will you choose to take a leap of faith and do something crazy—something so big, only God can make it happen?

You will never be able to look away again. Your eyes have been opened, and you will see the generation of fatherless sons wherever you go. I am not sorry that I awakened you. I rejoice that you have listened and looked, even though what there is to hear and see is an ugly mess created by human flesh. You are wide awake now and the enemy is afraid. For you are carrying the answer. Jesus is within you and it is your moment to come into unity with His purposes. It is your destiny to storm the gates of hell with the Heart of the Father. It is your purpose to rescue the lost children of this dark world. Will you turn on the light in that darkness? Will you courageously father a fatherless generation? Let us do it together.

Sing praises to God and to his name!
Sing loud praises to him who rides the clouds.
His name is the Lord—
rejoice in his presence!
Father to the fatherless, defender of widows—
this is God, whose dwelling is holy.
God places the lonely in families;
he sets the prisoners free and gives them joy.
But he makes the rebellious live in a sun-scorched land.

Psalm 68:4-6 (NLT)

Bibliography

Strong, James. *The New Strong's Exhaustive Concordance of the Bible: With Main Concordance, Appendix to the Main Concordance, Topical Index to the Bible, Dictionary of the Greek Testament*. Nashville: T. Nelson, 1990.

Trump, Donald J. "State of the Union Address." Address, State of the Union, United States Congress, Washington, D.C., February 5, 2019.

United States. Department of Health and Human Services. *The AFCARS Report*. Washington, D.C.: U.S. Dept. of Health and Human Services, Administration for Children and Families, Administration on Children, Youth and Families, Children's Bureau.

Freeman, Mitch. "Father Facts 7 (Download)." FatherSource™. 2015. Accessed May 01, 2019. https://store.fatherhood.org/father-facts-7-download/.

United States. US Department of Health and Human Services. Washington, DC. *Parenting a Child Who Has Experienced Trauma. Washington*, D.C.